THE BEST OF GASTON

Lenôtre's

DESSERTS

**Glorious Desserts from France's
Finest Pastry Maker**

Translated and Adapted by
Philip and Mary Hyman

Photos by Pierre Ginet

BARRON'S

Woodbury, New York • London • Toronto • Sydney

All inquiries should be addressed to:
Barron's Educational Series, Inc.
113 Crossways Park Drive
Woodbury, New York 11797

International Standard Book No. 0-8120-2450-8

PRINTED IN HONG KONG

3456   490   9 8 7 6 5 4 3 2 1

CONTENTS

PREFACE

Gaston Lenôtre is not only one of France's finest pastry chefs, he is one of the world's best teachers as well. With his daughter, Sylvie Gille-Naves, he has succeeded in writing recipes that are clear and easy to follow; even beginners will soon be producing splendid desserts that rival (or surpass) the productions of professional bakers.

The recipes in this book first appeared in LENÔTRE'S DESSERTS AND PASTRIES and LENÔTRE'S ICE CREAMS AND CANDIES, both available from Barron's. The present book contains recipes typically "Lenôtre," representing basically all the types of desserts explored in the previous books. Here, in one volume, is the *essential* Lenôtre as well as the best. Each chapter is a self-contained lesson on how to make and use the doughs and batters which are the cornerstones of French pastry. In addition to the chapters on pastry, special chapters are devoted to ice creams and sherbets — made the French way — including sundaes and frozen desserts created or personalized by Lenôtre after many years of experimentation.

Each recipe is preceded by either one, two, or three chef's hats (🎩). These indicate the potential difficulty of preparing the recipe. Those which are simple enough for even an inexperienced cook are preceded by one chef's hat (🎩), those which are a little more elaborate, but should not be too difficult for most cooks, by two chef's hats (🎩 🎩), whereas recipes requiring special skill and attention (even experienced cooks may have to make them several times to master the techniques) are indicated by three chef's hats (🎩 🎩 🎩). The chef's hats do *not* have anything to do with the quality of the recipe — they simply forewarn the reader that certain recipes are more elaborate or complicated than others. Beginners should start with the one-chef's-hat recipes and work their way up gradually to the three-hat preparations. If you read the instructions carefully, familiarize yourself with the Dictionary of Terms and Procedures, and don't attempt too complicated desserts until you are "ready" for them, you are sure to succeed. Your desserts will soon be like the stunning creations shown in the photographs throughout this book — the best of Gaston Lenôtre's desserts will soon be your best desserts too.

Philip and Mary Hyman

DICTIONARY OF TERMS AND PROCEDURES

Compiled by
Philip and Mary Hyman

Bain-marie: This is a French term used when a substance in one container is placed in another which contains hot water for cooking. The effect is that produced by using a double boiler. Some desserts, however, are baked in the oven in a "bain-marie"—in this case the mold containing the dessert is placed in a platter large enough to hold both the mold itself and enough boiling water to come half way up the side of the mold. It is easiest to measure the amount of water needed ahead of time, bring it to a boil on top of the stove, place the dessert in the oven-proof platter, pour in the boiling water and bake.

Baking: All pastry should be baked in the center of the oven unless otherwise indicated. To speed glazing, pastry can be placed closer to the top of the oven toward the end of the baking time. Some recipes call for the oven door to be kept ajar during baking. To do this, a wooden spoon is simply left wedged between the door and the oven, leaving an opening of about one inch between the top of the oven door and the oven. (See PREHEATING and BAKING SHEET)

Baking Sheet: Several baking sheets are sometimes necessary (e.g., a large quantity of cookies is baked in consecutive batches). *The baking sheet should always be cold before it goes into the oven.* Remove the baking sheet before preheating the oven; always dress pastry, meringues, etc., on a cold baking sheet. When buttering or buttering and flouring a baking sheet, follow the instructions given under MOLDS AND PANS for buttering and flouring these utensils. A good baking sheet should be made of metal that is thick enough not to buckle when heated. Most baking sheets are thin and buckle, so it is often a good idea to buy a baking sheet from a professional supply house, or have one cut to the size of your oven, if necessary, to avoid this inconvenience. It

1

is always better to bake only one baking sheet at a time, otherwise the baking may be uneven. Nevertheless, two cakes can often be baked on the same sheet, and this should be done whenever it is possible. (See BAKING)

Bowls: Pastry cooks in France often use the flat-bottomed metal mixing bowls pictured with the utensils (see photo page 9). These are not indispensable; china, porcelain, glass, or earthenware bowls will do. Whenever a large bowl is called for, this means that one full almost to the brim holds 3 quarts (3 liters); a medium-sized bowl holds 2 quarts (2 liters); and a small bowl holds 1 quart (1 liter) of water.

Bowls with covers that make them airtight are best for storage, but an ordinary bowl covered with aluminum foil is a good substitute.

Butter: Only the best unsalted butter should be used in these recipes. No substitutes for butter should ever be used. When butter is "softened" (or soft) this means that it is just soft enough to squeeze easily (usually an hour out of the refrigerator is sufficient).

Caramelized Almonds (Nut Brittle): Powdered caramelized almonds (called *praliné* in French) are often used to flavor and decorate desserts. (See Recipe 132).

Chestnut Cream and Chestnut Paste: Chestnut cream is made from fresh chestnuts, peeled and boiled with milk, sugar, and a little vanilla, then mashed to form a sweet thick cream. It is sold canned in some specialty shops. In French, it is called *crème de marrons*.

Chestnut paste (*pâte de marrons* in French) is a similar preparation, but it is much more compact than chestnut cream, being closer to the consistency of almond paste. It is generally less available than chestnut cream. Chestnut cream can sometimes be used instead of chestnut paste; this usually involves adjusting the measurements of the ingredients with which it is mixed, otherwise the resulting mixture will be too soft. (These adjustments are indicated in recipes where this substitution can be made.)

Cocoa Powder: This is also labeled as unsweetened cocoa, pure cocoa, or bitter cocoa powder depending on the brand; it is always one hundred percent cocoa—no sugar added—and it is always a powder.

Crème fraîche: Crème fraîche is nothing more than natural heavy (whipping) cream in which the lactic acid is allowed to act until the cream thickens almost to the consistency of mayonnaise. Pasteurization prevents this reaction from taking place. In almost all recipes calling for crème fraîche, heavy cream can be used with equally good results. The choice of one over the other is basically one of taste, crème fraîche having a taste vaguely reminiscent of hazelnuts. Good, fresh crème fraîche does not have a sour taste, although it will eventually turn into "sour cream" if allowed to sit long enough.

If desired, 1 cup of crème fraîche can be made by placing 1 cup fresh heavy cream in a saucepan, stir in 2 tablespoons buttermilk and heat until lukewarm to the touch—82 to 86°F (28 to 30°C) on a yoghurt thermometer. Allow to stand in a warm place—about 75°F (24°C)—for approximately 6 to 10 hours. The crème fraîche is ready when it is quite thick on top but liquid underneath—this will be discovered by stirring. Do not let the crème thicken too much at this stage or it will sour. When the crème has reached this stage, place it in a jar, stir it, cover the jar, and place in the refrigerator for at least 6 hours before using. The crème will thicken when it is chilled. Crème fraîche will keep refrigerated for about 1 week before it starts to go sour.

Cutting Dough: Often dough is rolled out and cut into different shapes with a sharp knife. When cutting some doughs, especially flaky pastry dough, the knife should simply be pressed straight down into the dough to cut it (like a cookie cutter). The knife should never be dragged through the dough since this presses the edges together and hinders its rising. Yeast doughs (e.g., brioche dough, etc.) on the other hand can be cut in the usual manner, but the dough should always be refrigerated before cutting for best results. In either case, a very large, extremely sharp straight-edged (not serrated) knife should be used.

Eggs: *All* the eggs used in this book should be medium. They should weigh approximately 1.75 oz. (49 g) or 21 oz. (596 g) a dozen. Since actual egg sizes may vary slightly, you should measure the volume of the eggs before using. If broken into a measuring cup, one beaten egg this size measures a scant ¼ cup (50 ml). If eggs of this size are not used, the measurements for eggs given in these recipes will have to be adjusted accordingly.

Egg Whites: Egg whites may be refrigerated (or frozen) for later use. When kept in a tightly closed jar they will keep in the refrigerator for 10 days or more. If they start to go bad they have an unpleasant odor that is easily recognizable. In these recipes 5 egg whites equal ¾ cup (155 g).

Egg whites are often beaten "until stiff." This means that the egg whites peak, and when held upright on the end of a beater or whisk, the peaks do not fall over. Egg whites should only be beaten just before they are to be used; they have to be folded into other ingredients rather than beaten in. (See FOLD)

Electric Mixer: Mixing times in this book are calculated for cooks using a mixer with only two or three speeds. Cooks using bigger and more sophisticated mixers (e.g., 8 to 10 speeds) should double the slow speed mixing times given here. Almost every recipe can be done with equal success by hand using a wire whisk. When a wire whisk is used, mixing times should be doubled.

Flan Rings: These are thin, smooth, metal circles of differing heights and diameters. They are used mainly by professional bakers in France. The ring is placed directly on the baking sheet and then lined with dough. After baking, the ring and tart are slid onto a rack to cool. The ring is removed by lifting it straight off of the tart or flan. Because there is nothing in between the bottom of the tart or flan dough and the baking sheet, the dough cooks quickly and evenly. Pie pans with removable bottoms are preferable when rings are unavailable.

3

Flour: Either all-purpose flour or pastry flour may be used in these recipes. *All measurements are for flour as it comes from the package.* If you wish to sift the flour, do so after measuring (see WEIGHTS AND MEASURES). Some flours absorb slightly more water than others. Sometimes it may be necessary to add extra liquid (a teaspoon at a time) when making certain doughs to achieve the desired consistency. All-purpose flour is preferable for doughs that contain yeast or baking powder. In the other recipes, either all-purpose or pastry flour, or a combination of both may be used.

Fold: This word is used primarily in connection with egg whites that have been beaten until very stiff. When beaten egg whites are to be mixed with other ingredients, they are "folded" in. This requires the use of a flat wooden spatula. Once the egg whites are in the same bowl as the ingredients they are to be mixed with, use the spatula to "cut" into the middle of the egg whites and scoop up, or fold over, half of the egg white mixture onto the other half. This cutting and folding should be done as carefully and quickly as possible. The airiness of the egg whites should not be lost, nor should particles of egg white remain in the final mixture, which should be absolutely homogenous.

Fondant: This is an opaque white icing preferred by French pastry chefs for glazing different cakes. It is shinier than ordinary icing, but when unavailable, an icing made by beating ⅔ cup (100 g) confectioners' sugar with 2 tablespoons of water can be used instead. Both this icing and fondant may be colored or flavored as desired. (See Recipe 16.)

Glaze: This procedure makes the surface of a cake or tart shiny.

Tarts, tartlets, and flans are most frequently glazed with apricot jam. The jam should not contain any pieces of fruit. It is heated until it melts in a sauce-pan, then "painted" over the surface of the dessert and allowed to cool. Only a small quantity of apricot jam is necessary for a large tart. Water may be mixed with the warm jam if it is too thick.

Another method of glazing, often used with cakes, is to sprinkle the surface of the cake with confectioners' sugar and place the cake under the broiler or in a hot oven for a short time. The confectioners' sugar becomes transparent and makes the cake shine. Often the sugar is sprinkled over the cake 10 minutes before the end of baking. Only enough sugar to lightly cover the surface of the cake is used.

Finally, many pastries are brushed with beaten egg or egg yolk before baking. This actually makes the pastry a more beautiful, even brown when baked, but can be considered a kind of glazing.

Layer Cakes: Génoise cakes often are cut in half, or into three or four layers after baking. To do this properly, you need a very long serrated knife and several strips of cardboard. It is essential that the blade of the knife be several inches longer than the diameter of the Génoise. Pile the cardboard strips on opposite sides of the Génoise so that they make two piles of equal height. The height of these piles is very important and depends on how many layers the cake has to be cut into. Use a ruler to measure the height of your Génoise. If you want to cut the cake into four equal layers, make the strips of cardboard into piles whose height is ¼ that of the Génoise (e.g., for a cake two inches tall, the piles of cardboard strips should be ½″ high). Place the blade of the knife flat against the two piles of cardboard strips and saw into the cake, keeping the knife in contact with the strips, which will guide the blade. Lift off the top section of the cake and remove this first, bottom slice from between the strips. Replace the remaining cake in between the cardboard strips and cut through the cake again. Repeat this procedure once more, and the Génoise will be cut into four equal layers.

Molds and Pans: When a specific size cake or pie pan is called for, the measurement given for it is for the diameter of the utensil measured across the top. Most molds used are made of aluminum, tin, or stainless steel. *When a mold or pan is buttered (or buttered and floured) before baking, measurements for these ingredients are not included in the list preceding the recipe.* To butter a mold for baking, simply rub the inside of the mold all over with butter until the walls and bottom of the mold are covered by a *light* film of butter. If the mold is to be floured as well, sprinkle in a little flour then, turning the mold constantly in all directions, shake the flour around until a thin even coating of flour has stuck to the butter. Empty out whatever flour does not adhere to the mold (the same procedure is followed with sugar instead of flour in some recipes).

Orange-Flower Water: This is a fragrant liquid produced by distilling orange blossoms. It is always used in very small doses and can be found in specialty shops (it is often used in North African and Middle Eastern cooking as well as French). If orange-flower water is unavailable, vanilla extract, though completely different in taste, may be used instead, if the recipe does not already call for vanilla in one form or another. If vanilla is already used, it is best not to add the vanilla extract. Orange-flower water is not indispensable. It can be omitted in most recipes where it is called for without harming the result.

Parchment Paper: Specially treated non-stick parchment paper is often used in Lenôtre's recipes. It is used to line baking sheets and pans to avoid sticking. If you prefer, you can simply grease the pan or baking sheet with butter instead of using parchment paper. Instructions are included in each recipe.

Pastry Bag: Pastry bags are either plastified (for easy cleaning) or made of cloth. Several different-sized bags and a complete set of nozzles are indispensable. To fill the bag (it is easier if two people do this), place the nozzle in the bag, then bend the bag just above the nozzle by placing the nozzle on its side on a table and lifting the open end of the bag upward, perpendicular to the nozzle. Spoon the cream or batter into the bag held in this position.

When squeezing out the batter onto a baking sheet, it is best to hold the nozzle with one hand, very close to, but not touching, the baking sheet. Squeeze the pastry bag as evenly as possible with the other hand. Squeeze very hard only toward the very end, when the bag appears to be empty—there is usually batter or cream left just behind the nozzle. Never use a syringe type decorator instead of a pastry bag—the results would be disastrous.

Plastic Scraper: This is a very small and useful utensil that is often used when making different doughs (see photo, page 10). Chopping the butter and flour together with the scraper keeps the butter from softening too much and speeds the mixing of these two ingredients. The rounded side of the scraper is used to scrape batter or dough from bowls when emptying them.

Powdered (ground) almonds: Powdered almonds are what one would think they are—almonds that have been ground to a powder. Sold commercially in France, they are more difficult to obtain in the United States. Almonds can be powdered in a food processor or blender—they will generally be somewhat pasty when freshly ground because of the oil in them. Use blanched almonds, or peel by parboiling 2 minutes, cooling, then removing the skins. Once ground, spread them out in a shallow dish and place in an oven at low heat for 1 to 2 hours—or leave them in a warm, dry place overnight. When dry, store the powdered almonds in a covered jar in a kitchen cabinet.

Preheating: It is indispensable that the oven be sufficiently preheated before baking. Fifteen or twenty minutes before anything is baked, the oven should be turned on and set to the temperature called for in each recipe.

Pricking Dough: Pastry dough is pricked with a fork or needle to prevent it from puffing up too much when baked. When pricking the dough, make sure the prongs of the fork (or the needle) go completely through the dough, and that the whole surface of the dough is evenly pricked. This is especially important when pricking flaky pastry.

Quantities: It is often advisable to make the largest quantities of those doughs which have to rise before baking (especially brioche dough). Smaller quantities can be made, but the dough is generally easier to work in large batches and it saves well.

Refrigeration: It is extremely important that many doughs be refrigerated before being rolled out. Most doughs need to be prepared a day ahead of time because of the refrigeration. Cold dough is preferably rolled out on a cold (marble) table, but it can be worked on any flat surface. If the dough is not sufficiently refrigerated, the large amount of butter in it will make it impossible to roll out. Unless otherwise indicated, whenever dough is called for in a list of ingredients, it should be cold (see basic recipes for different doughs).

Ribbon: This term is used when a batter falls from a spoon or whisk in a smooth stream and piles up on itself like a ribbon before sinking into the rest of the batter.

Rum: Dark rum is traditionally used in French pastry. The best dark, 90 proof rum is to be preferred in making these recipes.

Spatula: Three kinds of spatulas are used in this book. One is a long, metal, flexible blade-spatula (see photo, page 10) and is used primarily in icing cakes. Another is made of wood, and has a large, rounded end that tapers down into a handle (see photo, page 11). The wooden spatula is primarily used when folding egg whites into other ingredients.

A third (not pictured) is the flexible rubber or plastic spatula, used for scraping creams, chocolate, and so on, out of mixing bowls to ensure that there is no waste.

Sugar Coffee Beans: These are candy coffee beans consisting of a hollow, hard, sugar shell filled with a coffee-flavored liquid. If these are not available from a confectionary supply house, a small raisin may be used for a different, but satisfying effect. For a more "exotic" taste, the raisins can be soaked for a ½ hour in rum and then patted dry in a towel before being used.

Thermometer: There are two types of thermometers called for in this book.

The first is a candy thermometer, used in making certain candies and any other preparation where cooking sugar is involved. It must be able to withstand temperatures as high as 392°F (200°C) without breaking.

The second is a yoghurt thermometer, used in controlling the temperature of melted chocolate. Any thermometer with a range of about 50 to 212°F (10 to 100°C) can be used. The important thing is that the middle range should fall between 75 and 95°F (24 and 35°C).

Table: It is essential that the table used for making pastry be perfectly flat. Any surface will do, although marble is traditionally considered the best. This is because marble is not only flat, but it cools quickly. Cold dough is best worked on a cold table, so ice trays are sometimes placed on the marble table top to cool it. The table should be absolutely clean before working on it (it is best to scrape the table with a rubber or plastic scraper while rolling out dough, and to flour the table often to avoid sticking).

Time: A clock, or wristwatch, is indispensable when making pastry. Precise times are given in these recipes as often as possible, but since neither stove nor utensils (or cooks!) are completely uniform, cooking times may have to be adjusted. Often, "signs" have been given to judge when something is ready (e.g., reached a certain consistency or color), and they are just as important as the times given for baking. Preparation times listed before each recipe are slightly arbitrary since an experienced cook works faster than a beginner; nevertheless, they give the reader some idea how long it takes to prepare a certain dessert.

Turn: This is a term used in connection with the rolling out of flaky pastry. To give the dough a turn means to roll it out into a long rectangle, then to fold it in thirds. Before rolling it out again, the folded pastry is given a quarter turn —hence the name. By turning the pastry in this way, the rolling pin will always roll in the direction of the fold in the pastry, never across it. Flaky pastry is usually given 6 turns (i.e., rolled out 6 times) before being rolled into its final shape.

Turn Out: This term is used throughout the book and always means to remove a finished dessert from the mold, pan, or ring it was prepared in. This is done either immediately after taking the dessert in question from the oven, once the dessert has been allowed to cool but is still warm, or after the dessert is completely cold. Individual recipes give precise instructions on this point.

Whenever a cake mold is used, the cake is turned out by placing a plate, larger in diameter than the cake itself, on top of the mold and in one quick motion, turning the cake "upside down." The result is that the cake is now on the plate and one can lift the mold up and off with no problem.

Sometimes, as in the recipe for Rolled Brioche with Candied Fruits, the operation described above results in the bottom of the dessert facing upwards. In this case another platter is placed on top of the dessert and the dessert is turned "upside down" once more before serving.

Whenever a tart is turned out, it is *never* turned upside down, since this would ruin the appearance of the fruit. Either a flan circle or pie pan with a removable bottom is used when cooking a tart (see FLAN CIRCLE). If this cannot be done, the tart should simply be served in the pan it cooked in (small tartlets can be lifted or slid out of their pans on to the serving platter).

Vanilla Sugar: This is vanilla-flavored sugar that is sold already prepared in France. It is better when prepared at home. To make it, you need one vanilla bean, 1⅓ cups (150 g) lump sugar, a pair of scissors, a mortar, and a pestle.

Hold the vanilla bean over the mortar and, using the scissors, cut it into tiny slices. Keep cutting until the entire vanilla bean has been sliced and has fallen into the mortar. Place half of the sugar in the mortar and begin pounding with the pestle. After about 10 minutes, pour the pounded vanilla and sugar into a very fine sieve and shake the sieve over a piece of waxed paper until all the finest pieces have gone through. Place what is left in the sieve back into the mortar, add the remaining sugar, and pound for another 10 minutes, then sift again. What remains in the sieve this time can be pounded once more, but no more sugar should be added. The vanilla sugar can be kept in an airtight container or tin for later use.

To make powdered vanilla, follow the instructions given here, but use only ½ cup (60 g) of sugar lumps instead of 1⅓ cups (150 g).

Vanilla sugar is seldom used in large quantities. If none is available, a few drops of vanilla extract can often be used instead.

Weights and Measures: The exact gram weights have been retained in parentheses in this book. Scales are inevitably more accurate than cups and tablespoons. When measuring in cups, the ingredient should never be packed in. The cup should be filled and shaken gently *only* to level the ingredient so that the measurement can be read easily. Ingredients such as butter should be placed in the cup so that no air bubbles or pockets remain, and the butter should be pressed until flat across the top. All spoon or cup measurements are level unless otherwise indicated. In referring to tablespoons or teaspoons, *generous* means that the contents of the spoon make a mound rather than being level with the edge of the spoon. *Scant* means that the spoon is not quite full, but approaches the measurement given. When applied to cup measurements, *generous* means that the contents of the cup are to come slightly above the line indicating the measurement given, but never more than 1 liquid ounce (⅛ cup) above it. *Scant* means that the contents are below the measurement given, but no more than 1 liquid ounce (⅛ cup) below it.

Whiten: When sugar is beaten with butter or egg yolks until very pale yellow, the mixture is said to whiten. This term is often used in conjunction with the term "form a ribbon" (see RIBBON).

Yeast: Compressed baker's yeast is to be preferred in the following recipes, however granulated dry yeast may be used instead. One cake of compressed baker's yeast equals one packet of granulated dry yeast.

Zest: This is a term used in connection with citrus fruits. The zest of an orange or lemon is the very thin, colored part of the peel, which can be removed either with a special utensil called a zester or with an ordinary vegetable peeler. The zest *never* includes the thick, whitish part of the peel.

The zest is used as a flavoring in several recipes. It is used either in strips and infused with a liquid or by being removed and finely chopped or else grated off the fruit with a fine-holed vegetable grater. If orange or lemon *peel* is called for, this means the entire peel including the thick white part.
thick white part. The whole peel is used notably in making Half-Candied Orange Peel (Recipe 167).

Photo Captions

Page 10:

1	Scale and weights
2	Plastic pastry cups
3	Paper pastry cups
4	Plastic scraper
5	Serrated knife
6	Metal mixing bowls
7	Paper doilies
8	Cookie cutter
9	Cake rack
10	Individual ribbed brioche molds
11	Petit four molds
12	Ribbed brioche mold
13	Pie tin for tartlet
14	Cake pan
15	Cookie molds
16	Non-stick parchment paper
17	Rolling pin
18	Sugar dredger
19	Putty knife
20	Flexible blade-spatula
21	Small ladle
22	Paring knife
23	Vegetable peeler
24	Cutting board
25	Orange or lemon peeler

Page 11

1	Flan circle
2	Round metal nozzles, 1/16″ (0.2 cm) to 3/4″ (2 cm)
3	Flat-toothed nozzle
4	Star-shaped nozzle
5	Skimmer
6	Oven
7	Wire whisk
8	Pound cake mold
9	Kugelhopf mold
10	Individual oval flan rings
11	Individual flan circle
12	Tartlet circle
13	Dough hook
14	Pastry bag
15	Pastry brush
16	10-speed mixer
17	Wooden spatulas and spoon
18	Candy thermometer
19	Measuring cup

Page 12

1	Scale
2	Plastic cup cake or baba cases
3	Metal frame with movable "ruler"
4	Flan ring
5	Tartlet ring
6	Ice cream scoop (3 tablespoon capacity)
7	Wooden spoon
8	Metal mixing bowl
9	Round metal nozzles ¹⁄₁₆ to ³⁄₄ inch (2 mm to 2 cm)
10	Star-shaped nozzle
11	Skimmer
12	Stainless steel wire whisk
13	Stainless steel pot
14	Timer
15	Plastic ice cream mold (square)
16	Plastic molds for frozen desserts (round)
17	Plastic molds for ice cream on a stick
18	Electric grater
19	Flexible-blade, metal spatula
20	Sieve
21	Pastry brush
22	Jam jar with screw-on lid
23	Sugar dredger
24	Electric mixer with several speeds
25	Food processor with blades
26	Rolling pin
27	Traditional ice–salt ice cream freezer
28	Freezer compartment ice cream freezer
29	Drum sieve
30	Candy thermometer
31	Measuring cup

Creams, Fillings, and Decorations

Baking is only one of the pastry chef's occupations. What is a genoise without a filling? an éclair without a cream? or a yule log without the traditional figurines? This chapter will teach you all of the basic fillings, icings, and decorations essential to the pastry chef's art and which lift plain cakes to the level of artistic creation. *Ed.*

1

Chantilly Cream

Chantilly cream (vanilla-flavored whipped cream) can be mixed with other creams to make them lighter; it can also be flavored with chocolate. Avoid whipping the cream for too long; otherwise it will turn into butter.

PREPARATION 10 minutes

INGREDIENTS *For 4 cups (570 g) Chantilly*
2 cups (450 g) crème fraîche, very cold
6 tablespoons (1 dl) cold milk
2 tablespoons (30 g) granulated sugar
1½ teaspoons (8 g) vanilla sugar
3 tablespoons (50 g) shaved ice or ice water

Or 2 cups, generous (500 ml), heavy cream
1½ teaspoons (8 g) vanilla sugar

For 2 cups (285 g) Chantilly
1 cup (225 g) crème fraîche, very cold
3 tablespoons (5 cl) cold milk
1 tablespoon (15 g) granulated sugar
¾ teaspoon (4 g) vanilla sugar
1½ tablespoons (25 g) shaved ice or ice water

Or 1 cup (250 ml) heavy cream
¾ teaspoon (4 g) vanilla sugar

UTENSILS Electric mixer
Large mixing bowl, chilled

13

Whipping the Cream: Mix the crème fraîche with the milk in a chilled mixing bowl; add the sugar, vanilla sugar, and the shaved ice or ice water, whip at low speed for one minute, then whip at high speed for 1 to 3 minutes more or until it stands in soft peaks.

If using heavy cream, simply whip it with the vanilla sugar in a chilled bowl until it peaks. No other ingredients are necessary.

Refrigerate the Chantilly for later use or use immediately. It may either be used as it is or added to other pastry creams to make them lighter.

Note: Be sure to have all your ingredients very cold before you start, or else you will run the risk of turning the cream into butter.

To Store: Chantilly cream keeps for 24 hours if refrigerated in a tightly closed container.

2

Vanilla Pastry Cream

This recipe can be used to prepare other flavors of pastry cream and as a garnish for many recipes.

PREPARATION	10 minutes
INGREDIENTS	*For 2⅓ cups (580 g) cream*
	2 cups (½ l) milk
	½ vanilla bean, split in half lengthwise
	6 egg yolks
	⅔ cup (150 g) granulated sugar
	4 tablespoons (40 g) flour *or* cornstarch
	For 1 cup, generous (290 g), cream
	1 cup (¼ l) milk
	¼ vanilla bean, split in half lengthwise
	3 egg yolks
	⅓ cup (75 g) granulated sugar
	2 tablespoons (20 g) flour *or* cornstarch
UTENSILS	Saucepan
	Wire whisk
	Electric mixer [optional]
	Mixing bowls

Making the Pastry Cream: Place the milk and split vanilla bean in a saucepan and bring to a boil. Cover and keep hot. With the wire whisk (or mixer on medium speed), beat the sugar and egg yolks together, until the mixture whitens and forms a ribbon; then gently stir in the cornstarch or flour with the whisk.

Strain out the vanilla bean and pour the hot milk into the egg and sugar mixture, beating all the while with the wire whisk. Pour the mixture back into the saucepan and bring to a boil again, stirring constantly with the wire whisk so that the mixture does not stick to the bottom of the saucepan. Boil for 1 minute, stirring vigorously, then pour into a bowl and lightly rub the surface of the cream with a lump of butter to keep a skin from forming as it cools.

3

Coffee Pastry Cream

Preparing the Pastry Cream: With a wooden spoon, stir 1½ tablespoons of instant coffee or 3 teaspoons coffee extract into 2⅓ cups (580 g) hot pastry cream.

4

Chocolate Pastry Cream

Preparing the Pastry Cream: Break 5½ ounces (160 g) of semi-sweet chocolate into small pieces and add to 2⅓ cups (580 g) of hot pastry cream. Let the chocolate melt, stirring occasionally with a wooden spoon to mix it into the cream.

To Store: These pastry creams will keep for a maximum of 2 days in the refrigerator in a tightly sealed container.

5

Almond Pastry Cream

Almond pastry cream is used to garnish tarts, brioche, and other desserts. The almond mixture can be prepared as much as a week ahead of time.

PREPARATION   15 minutes, plus 20 minutes to prepare the pastry cream

INGREDIENTS   *For approximately 5½ cups (1 kg) cream*
1½ cups (375 g) pastry cream (Recipe 2)
2 cups (250 g) powdered almonds
1⅔ cups (250 g) confectioners' sugar
3 eggs
2½ tablespoons (25 g) cornstarch
1½ tablespoons (25 ml) rum
1 cup, generous (250 g), soft butter

For approximately 2¾ cups (500 g) cream
¾ cup (185 g) pastry cream (Recipe 2)
1 cup (125 g) powdered almonds
¾ cup, generous (125 g), confectioners' sugar
1½ eggs, beaten
4 teaspoons (12 g) cornstarch
2½ teaspoons (12 ml) rum
¼ pound (125 g) soft butter

UTENSILS   Electric mixer with paddle, or wooden spoon
Mixing bowl

Making the Cream: Prepare the pastry cream (Recipe 2) one hour ahead of time if you are planning to make the almond pastry cream the same day.

In the mixing bowl, cream the butter until soft, add the almond powder, beating until well mixed, then add the confectioners' sugar. Beat in the eggs one by one. Blend with the mixer set at medium speed until the batter is light and smooth, then add the cornstarch and the rum.

Add the chilled pastry cream to the almond base, mixing in one tablespoon at a time until blended.

To Store: Almond pastry cream will keep for up to 8 days in the refrigerator if stored in a tightly sealed container.

6

Chocolate Mousse

Chocolate mousse may be eaten as it is, or decorated with chocolate shavings and confectioners' sugar. It may also be used as a filling for other desserts.

PREPARATION   15 minutes

INGREDIENTS   *For approximately 2 cups (300 g) mousse (serves 6)*
                     4½ ounces (125 g) semi-sweet chocolate
                     ⅓ cup (75 g) butter, broken into pieces
                     2 egg yolks
                     3 egg whites = ½ cup (90 g)
                     1½ tablespoons (20 g) granulated sugar

UTENSILS   Double boiler
                     Mixing bowl
                     Electric mixer
                     Wooden spoon
                     Wooden spatula
                     Pastry bag with star-shaped nozzle [optional]

Making the Mousse: Melt the chocolate in a double boiler. Remove from the heat and add the butter, stirring it in with a wooden spoon. Allow the mixture to cool completely—it should be the consistency of a very thick cream—then stir in the egg yolks one by one.

Beat the egg whites until very stiff; halfway through, add the sugar. Fold the chocolate mixture into the egg whites with the wooden spatula, making sure the two elements are perfectly blended together.

Serving: If you are serving the mousse plain, pour into individual molds or into a deep bowl. It may be decorated by putting some of the mousse through a pastry bag set with a star-shaped nozzle. Chocolate shavings can be made with a vegetable peeler if desired. In any case, serve the mousse very cold, accompanied with a slice of brioche or petits fours.

$\underline{\underline{\textstyle\text{\small{W}}}}$

7

Butter Cream

This filling can be used as it is or flavored with chocolate, coffee, liqueur, etc. as shown in the following recipes.

PREPARATION   15 minutes

INGREDIENTS   *For approximately 2⅔ cups (500 g) cream*
¾ cup, generous (200 g), granulated sugar
⅓ cup (8 cl) water
8 egg yolks
1 cup (250 g) soft butter, broken into pieces

   Optional French Meringue (see Recipe 79 for procedure)
3 egg whites = ½ cup (100 g)
3½ tablespoons (50 g) granulated sugar
⅓ cup (50 g) confectioners' sugar

For approximately 1⅓ cups (250 g) cream
½ cup, scant (100 g), granulated sugar
2½ tablespoons (4 cl) water
4 egg yolks
½ cup (125 g) soft butter, broken into pieces
   Optional French Meringue (see Recipe 79 for procedure)
2 small egg whites = ¼ cup (55 g)
5 teaspoons (25 g) granulated sugar
2½ tablespoons (25 g) confectioners' sugar

UTENSILS   Small heavy-bottomed saucepan
Candy thermometer [optional]
Mixing bowl
Electric mixer or wire whisk

Preparing the Sugar: Boil the sugar with the water in a small saucepan until it reaches 250°F (120°C); this should take no more than 10 minutes. Use the thermometer or test the sugar by letting a drop fall from a spoon into a glass of cold water. If the temperature is correct, the sugar will form a ball and hold its shape on the bottom of the glass.

Making the Cream: Meanwhile, whip the egg yolks at medium speed in a mixing bowl, then add the boiling sugar little by little, being careful not to let it fall on the sides of the bowl or the beaters. Continue beating until the mixture is cool (2 to 3 minutes). When the cream is cool, add the butter and continue to whip the mixture at low speed for 5 more minutes. At this point, add the desired flavoring or, if you wish a lighter cream, fold in the French Meringue.

To Store: Unflavored butter cream filling will keep refrigerated for up to 8 days in a tightly closed container. Before using the cream, let it stand for 1

18

hour at room temperature and then work the cream with a wooden spatula until it is smooth before adding a desired flavoring.

♔

8

Coffee-Flavored Butter Cream

Preparing the Cream: Dissolve 1½ tablespoons of instant coffee in 2 teaspoons of hot water or, if you prefer, use 2 teaspoons of coffee extract and add it to 2⅔ cups (500 g) butter cream filling.

♔

9

Chocolate Butter Cream

Preparing the Cream: Mix 5½ ounces (160 g) of melted sweet chocolate to 2⅔ cups (500 g) butter cream filling.

♔

10

Almond Butter Cream

Preparing the Cream: Add ⅔ cup, scant (100 g), of powdered candied almonds to 2⅔ cups (500 g) butter cream filling.

11

Dessert Syrup

PREPARATION   5 minutes

INGREDIENTS

For 1 cup (2½ dl) syrup
⅔ cup (1½ dl) water
½ cup, generous (135 g), granulated sugar
Flavorings—3 tablespoons (½ dl) alcohol of your choice:
    Kirsch, rum, Grand Marnier, etc. *or* 3 tablespoons
    (½ dl) water mixed with ¾ teaspoon vanilla extract
    or coffee extract

For ⅔ cup (1.5 dl) syrup
6 tablespoons (9 cl) water
⅓ cup (80 g) granulated sugar
Flavorings—2 tablespoons (3 cl) alcohol of your choice:
    Kirsch, rum, Grand Marnier, etc. *or* 2 tablespoons
    (3 cl) water mixed with ½ teaspoon vanilla extract
    or coffee extract

UTENSILS

Saucepan
Wooden spoon

Making the Syrup: Place the water and sugar in a saucepan and bring to a boil, stirring until the sugar is dissolved. Remove from the heat. When cool, add the flavoring of your choice.

This syrup is generally used lukewarm or cold.

To Store: Dessert syrup will keep for several weeks in the refrigerator in a tightly closed container.

12

Vanilla Sauce

This sauce is used with many desserts. Rich in egg yolks, it is also the base for Bavarian creams and charlottes.

PREPARATION	15 minutes
COOLING TIME	30 minutes
INGREDIENTS	*For 2⅔ cups (6 dl) sauce* 2 cups (½ l) milk 1 vanilla bean, split lengthwise 6 egg yolks ⅔ cup (150 g) granulated sugar
	For 1⅓ cups (3 dl) sauce 1 cup (¼ l) milk ½ vanilla bean, split lengthwise 3 egg yolks ⅓ cup (75 g) granulated sugar
UTENSILS	Saucepan Wooden spatula Electric mixer or wire whisk Mixing bowl Bowl filled with cold water

Making the Sauce: Place the milk and vanilla bean in a saucepan and bring to a boil. Lower the heat, cover the pot and let the vanilla bean infuse for 10 minutes.

Beat the egg yolks and the sugar on medium speed until the mixture whitens and forms a ribbon. Still beating, add the milk to the egg yolks. Pour the mixture back into the saucepan. Heat slowly, stirring constantly with a wooden spatula; do not allow the mixture to boil. When the liquid coats the spatula, remove the saucepan from the heat and immediately place the pan in a bowl of cold water to stop the cooking. Remove the vanilla bean.

Should the sauce accidentally come to a boil and separate, pour it into a blender and blend it at high speed, or pour a little of it at a time into a bottle, and shake vigorously.

Cool the mixture by leaving the pot in the bowl of cold water for about 30 minutes. Whip the sauce with a whisk from time to time while it is cooling.

Chocolate Sauce

Serve cold as a sauce with a charlotte, a soufflé, or a brioche. This sauce can also be served hot, on top of glazed cream puffs or vanilla ice cream.

PREPARATION

15 minutes

INGREDIENTS

For approximately 2 cups (½ l) sauce
9 ounces (250 g) semi-sweet chocolate
1 cup (2.5 dl) milk
5 teaspoons crème fraîche *or* heavy cream
¼ cup (60 g) granulated sugar
2½ tablespoons (35 g) butter

For approximately ¾ cup (2 dl) sauce
3½ ounces (100 g) semi-sweet chocolate
6½ tablespoons (1 dl) milk
2 teaspoons crème fraîche *or* heavy cream
5 teaspoons (25 g) granulated sugar
1 tablespoon (15 g) butter

UTENSILS

Double boiler
Wooden spatula
Saucepan

Making the Sauce: Melt the chocolate in the double boiler. Meanwhile, bring the milk to a boil, add the crème fraîche and bring back to a boil.

Remove the pot from the heat, then stir in the sugar, the melted chocolate, and the butter. Replace the pot on the fire and boil the sauce for a few seconds, then pour into a bowl and allow to cool.

Fresh Fruit Sauce

This sauce can be served with a brioche, Génoise cake, charlotte, pudding, or Bavarian cream.

PREPARATION   10 minutes

INGREDIENTS   *For approximately 4⅓ cups (1 l) sauce*
2¼ pounds (1 kg) fresh fruit
2⅔ cups (600 g) granulated sugar

For approximately 2 cups, generous (½ l), sauce
1 pound 2 ounces (500 g) fresh fruit
1⅓ cups (300 g) granulated sugar

UTENSILS   Electric blender

Making the Sauce: Use any fruit of your choice, such as peaches, apricots, strawberries, raspberries, etc. Cut large fruits into quarters. Add the fruit to the sugar and blend at medium speed for 2 minutes, or until the ingredients are blended together well.

Note: When fruit is out of season, you can use canned fruit; just drain off the syrup and blend as described above, omitting the sugar.

To Store: Fruit sauce will keep for up to 8 days in a tightly closed container in the refrigerator. This sauce can also be frozen. When thawing, whip the sauce to make it smooth again.

♛

15

Chocolate Icing

This icing can be made easily and is a good substitute for chocolate fondant icing. It is shiny, but soft; be careful not to touch the cake with your fingers once it is iced.

PREPARATION   10 minutes

INGREDIENTS   *For 1½ cups (450 g) icing, sufficient for 2 cakes, each serving 6 persons*
7 ounces (200 g) semi-sweet chocolate
5 tablespoons (80 g) butter
4 tablespoons cold water
1 cup (160 g) confectioners' sugar

For ¾ cups (225 g) icing, sufficient for 1 cake serving 6 persons
3½ ounces (100 g) semi-sweet chocolate
2½ tablespoons (40 g) butter
2 tablespoons cold water
½ cup (80 g) confectioners' sugar

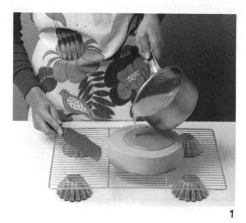

1

2

Wooden spatula
             Small mixing bowl
             Flexible blade-spatula
             Flat rack
             Sieve
             Saucepan

Making the Icing: Sift the sugar. Heat the chocolate in a double boiler until melted, then add the sifted sugar and the butter, cut into pieces. Stir until smooth, then remove the saucepan from the heat and add the water, one tablespoon at a time, to cool the mixture. This icing must be lukewarm to ice the cake. If it is too hot, it will run off; if it is too cold, it will not spread easily.

Icing the Cake: Place your cake on a plate that is smaller than the cake itself, then place on a rack. Spread the icing evenly on the cake, using the spatula (see photos 1 and 2).

16

Fondant Icing

PREPARATION   **10 minutes**

INGREDIENTS   *For 1 cup (350 g) icing, sufficient for 1 cake serving 6 persons*
                 1 cup (350 g) plain fondant
                 4 teaspoons cold dessert syrup (Recipe 11)
                 3 to 4 drops food coloring: coffee extract, carmine, red,
                    yellow, *or* green

UTENSILS   Double boiler
                 Flexible blade-spatula
                 Wooden spatula
                 Rack

Making the Icing: In a double boiler, melt the fondant until barely lukewarm. Stir in the dessert syrup, then add the food coloring, drop by drop so as to control the color. If you do not have coffee extract, dissolve 2 teaspoons of instant coffee in a little bit of water, then add the coffee to the syrup.

Icing the Cake: Ice the cake using the technique given for chocolate icing, Recipe 15.

17

Walnut–Almond Paste

PREPARATION   20 minutes

INGREDIENTS   *For approximately 2 cups, tightly packed (500 g)*
1 generous cup (110 g) walnut meats
Generous ⅔ cup (110 g) blanched almonds
1²/₃ cup (250 g) confectioners' sugar
1 small egg white, lightly beaten

UTENSILS   Food processor *or* electric blender
Mixing bowl
Electric mixer with paddle, wooden spoon, *or* spatula

Making the Walnut–Almond Paste: Place a third each of the walnut meats, almonds, and confectioner's sugar in the food processor or blender and grind, adding the egg white, little by little. Add no more than a third of the egg white to each batch. When a fine paste is formed, place it in a mixing bowl and proceed in the same way with the other two-thirds of the ingredients. If using a food processor, you may make all the paste at once if your machine is large enough.

When all the walnut–almond paste has been placed in the bowl, beat it until smooth with an electric mixer equipped with a paddle or by hand with a wooden spoon or spatula. If the mixture seems too soft and sticky, add more confectioners' sugar. If too crumbly and dry, add more egg white. Allow to rest for 1 to 2 hours before using.

18

Homemade Almond Paste

INGREDIENTS   *For approximately 1 pound 2 ounces (500 g) paste*
1½ cups (200 g) powdered almonds
1⅔ cups (250 g) confectioners' sugar
2 egg whites from small eggs

Making the Paste: Mix the almond powder with the confectioners' sugar, then add the egg whites and blend until smooth.

Almond Paste Decorations

Cakes, especially Génoise cakes, and other pastries may be topped with almond paste. Almond paste may also be used to make holly leaves and other decorations for Yule logs.

PREPARATION	**Variable**
INGREDIENTS	*For 1 cake, serving 6 persons* 9 ounces (250 g) almond paste (Recipe 18) ⅔ cup (100 g) confectioners' sugar (approximately), to dust table 3 drops food coloring (approximately) for pastel colors
UTENSILS	Rolling pin Knife

Preparing the Almond Paste: Mix the almond paste with the food coloring by working the paste as you would modeling clay. Add more food coloring if you wish the color to be more intense. Continue working the paste until it is of a uniform color.

Dust the surface of your work table with confectioners' sugar. Roll out the colored almond paste, turning the dough every time you roll it to keep it from sticking to the table, and dusting with more confectioners' sugar if necessary. If the dough should stick to the table and break, just pick it up, pack it into a ball and roll it out again.

Decorating the Cake: A cake must be covered with a thin layer of dessert cream—such as pastry cream—before being topped with almond paste. When this has been done, roll out the almond paste into a circle, then roll it around the rolling pin. Unroll it over the cake, as you would when lining a pie pan. To make the paste stick to the cake, press it gently with the palm of your hand against the surface of the cake, being careful not to wrinkle it.

Cut off the excess dough with a knife.

To make holly leaves, cut out the leaves with the point of a sharp knife, then twist the ends of the leaves slightly. To make green moss, press the paste through a sieve, held over a plate. With the blade of a knife, pick up the moss carefully, placing it on the surface of the cake, tapping it *very* lightly with the tips of your fingers to make it stick to the pastry cream.

Swiss Meringue Decorations

Swiss meringue is used to make decorations, including snowmen, mushrooms, and Doigts de Fée (Chocolate Fingers).

PREPARATION	15 minutes
BAKING TIME	45 minutes
INGREDIENTS	4 egg whites = ⅔ cup (120 g) 1⅔ cups (250 g) confectioners' sugar *or* 1 cup, generous (250 g), granulated sugar Unsweetened powdered cocoa [optional] ¾ cup (120 g) powdered semi-sweet chocolate [optional]
UTENSILS	Large mixing bowl Large pot Electric mixer Thermometer Wire whisk Pastry bag with ¼″ (0.6 cm) nozzle Parchment paper Baking sheets

The Batter: Preheat the oven to 275°F (135°C). Place the egg whites and sugar in a large mixing bowl and set the bowl over a large pot of boiling water; the water should not touch the bowl. Beat the egg whites and the sugar with the whisk until the mixture reaches 120°F (50°C). Remove from the heat and beat with the mixer at high speed for 5 minutes, then lower the speed and beat for 5 more minutes or until the meringue is very stiff. Fit the pastry bag with the nozzle; fill with the batter. Butter the baking sheet and dust it with flour or line it with parchment paper, sticking each corner to the sheet with a dab of meringue.

Squeeze the meringue onto the baking sheet in long strips or various shapes, such as mushroom caps and stems.

Note: If you wish, sprinkle the meringues with powdered unsweetened cocoa. Chocolate meringue can be made by adding the powdered semi-sweet chocolate while beating the egg whites at high speed.

Baking: Bake the meringues for 40 to 50 minutes in the oven, keeping the oven door ajar with a spoon. Taste a piece; it should be dry on the outside and soft inside. When baked, attach the stems to the mushroom caps by pressing them together gently. Cut the long strips into ½″ (1 cm) pieces to make Doigts de Fée (Chocolate Fingers), and into 1½″ (4 cm) pieces for petits fours (see photo 23, page 136).

To Store: Swiss meringue will keep for 3 weeks in a tightly closed box in a dry place.

21

Chocolate Palms and Other Chocolate Ornaments

PREPARATION	1 hour
COOLING TIME	15 minutes per strip
INGREDIENTS	*For 8 to 10 chocolate palms* 7 ounces (200 g) semi-sweet chocolate 2 teaspoons vegetable shortening
UTENSILS	A sheet of ordinary writing or typing paper Pencil Ruler Transparent plastic sheet approximately 8 × 12 inches (20 × 30 cm) Scissors A piece of nonstick parchment paper Double boiler *or* mixing bowl and saucepan (*bain-marie*) Wooden spoon Yoghurt thermometer Box with cover (for storing)

Making the Chocolate Palms: On a piece of paper, use a pen or pencil to draw a palm tree that is no more than 4 inches (10 cm) tall; don't make the trunk of the tree too narrow, otherwise it will break too easily when the chocolate hardens (see photo).

Take a sheet of plastic (the kind used for making "sleeves" or folders for protecting documents or any other fairly thick plastic) and cut it into three strips 8 × 4 inches (20 × 10 cm).

Place the drawing of the palm on a flat surface and cover it with one end of the strip of plastic.

Make a "pastry bag" by rolling a piece of nonstick parchment paper into a cone shape. Use a piece of tape to attach the edges of the paper where they overlap. The tip of the cone should be quite pointed, and the whole thing made neatly so that when the melted chocolate is poured into it, it will not leak out.

Heat the chocolate and shortening in a double boiler or a *bain-marie*, using a yoghurt thermometer to be sure that the temperature does not exceed 95°F (35°C). Once the chocolate and shortening have melted, mix them together and pour the mixture into the paper "pastry bag."

Hold the bag near the drawing of the palm and cut off the very tip of the paper cone, making a tiny hole so that the chocolate will flow out in a thin but even stream. As it does so, use it to draw around the outside edges of your palm tree, on the plastic; then fill in the middle of your chocolate "drawing" until you have a solid chocolate palm. Carefully slide the plastic over to reveal the drawing on the paper again, and make another chocolate palm in the same manner; generally you can make 3 to 4 chocolate palms on each strip of plastic.

Once the palms on any strip of plastic are completed, place the plastic immediately in the refrigerator so that the palms on it can harden. Then continue making palms in the same way on the other strips of plastic.

Wait no longer than 15 minutes once the chocolate has been refrigerated before checking it to see if it has hardened enough to handle. If it has, place the palms immediately into a tightly closing container, where they should be kept until wanted.

To Store: Chocolate palms can be kept refrigerated in a tightly closed container for up to 2 weeks.

Other Decorations: Other chocolate ornaments can be made in the same way as the palms: chocolate swans, stars, or christmas trees are only a few of the ideas you might like to try. Once the technique of working with the chocolate in this way is mastered, whole scenes can be drawn and used to decorate the tops of frozen desserts.

Note: Once the palms (or other chocolate ornaments) have hardened in the refrigerator, they can be decorated with little dots or lines of white chocolate, squeezed from the "pastry bag" in the same way as the dark chocolate.

22

Cooking Sugar

Cooking sugar is a delicate operation which requires a great deal of attention. When making jams, caramels, syrups, and confectioneries in general, sugar must be cooked to very specific densities. Before thermometers became widespread, the only way to check the evolution of the sugar as it cooked was to quickly dip the thumb and index finger into a bowl of ice water, then into the cooking syrup, and back into the water; the sugar would "thread" between the fingers, form into a soft ball, a hard ball, etc. This method is demonstrated in the following photos, dropping the syrup into the water from a spoon rather than using the fingers.

Today, most people use a candy thermometer when cooking sugar, and this is what we recommend. In the table, therefore, temperatures are listed which correspond to the various stages the sugar goes through as it cooks. Remember that candy thermometers are not perfectly exact, and that they can vary by 3° to 4°F (2°C). Be sure that your thermometer never touches the bottom or sides of the pan in which you are cooking the sugar; as a general rule, it is better to cook the sugar slightly more than the degree marked on the thermometer to assure that the correct temperature has indeed been reached.

The table on pages 34-35 lists how each type of cooked sugar is principally used in modern confectionery. Ed.

PREPARATION	5 minutes
COOKING TIME	5 to 15 minutes
INGREDIENTS	2½ cups (500 g) granulated sugar ⅔ cup (1½ dl) water 10 drops lemon juice
UTENSILS	Medium, heavy-bottomed saucepan (preferably stainless steel) Wooden spoon *or* spatula Skimmer Small bowl Ordinary teaspoon Pastry Brush Candy thermometer (optional)

Cooking the Sugar: Place the sugar and water in a heavy-bottomed saucepan and set over moderate heat. If cooking with gas, make sure that the flame does not go beyond the edges of the saucepan.

Fill a small bowl with cold water and a few ice cubes and place it, as well as an ordinary teaspoon, on a table or other surface next to the saucepan.

Heat the syrup, stirring with a wooden spoon or spatula; then, just before it boils, stir in the lemon juice. As soon as the syrup boils, stop stirring, but clean the sides of the saucepan with a clean, moist pastry brush; any impurities contained in the sugar will rise to the surface and stick to the sides of the pot. Continue cooking the sugar using the following table to determine when it has reached the desired stage.

3.   257°F (125°C) Hard Ball

4.   311°F (155°C) Very Hard Crack

5.   320°F (160°C) Light Caramel

6.   356°F (180°C) Dark Caramel

1.   223°F (106°C) Thread

2.   224°F (118°C) Firm Ball

| Name | Temperature | | Aspect and *Uses* |
	°F	°C	
GLOSS	214°	101°	The surface of the syrup is covered with large bubbles.
LARGE GLOSS	217°	103°	The bubbles become much smaller.

For the following stages it will be necessary to take a little syrup out of the saucepan with the teaspoon. With a sharp downward movement, shake the teaspoon so that the syrup falls in the bowl of ice water; then lift it out of the water with your thumb and index finger. Change the water in the bowl every time you make a test because the syrup must fall into pure, very cold, water.

THREAD	223°	106°	Little sticky threads will form as you separate your thumb and index finger. (Photo 1) *Final cooking of jams.*
BLOW	228/234°	109/112°	Dip a skimmer into the syrup; then lift it out and blow hard through the holes—little bubbles of sugar will form. *Syrup for jams and black currant liqueur.*
SOFT BALL	239°	115°	A very soft, flattened ball can be formed with the syrup. *Certain jams.*
FIRM BALL	244°	118°	The ball is firmer, but still somewhat soft—it holds its shape better. (Photo 2) *Caramelized Almonds and Hazelnuts, nut brittle powder and paste.*
HARD BALL	257/275°	125/135°	The ball is quite hard and perfectly round (Photo 3) *Soft caramels—257° (125°)— Italian meringue and butter cream used in pastries.*

Name	Temperature °F	°C	Aspect and *Uses*
LIGHT CRACK	277/286°	136/141°	The syrup detaches itself from the fingers and sticks to the teeth when chewed.
HARD CRACK	293/302°	145/150°	The film of sugar breaks easily but still sticks to the teeth.
VERY HARD CRACK	311/315°	155/157°	The film of sugar breaks like glass and no longer sticks to the teeth. (Photo 4) *Nougatine, sugar-coated fruit candies, spun sugar.*
LIGHT CARAMEL	320°	160°	The sugar turns a light golden brown color. (Photo 5) *For caramelizing cream puff pastries and decorative pastry centerpieces.*
DARK CARAMEL	356°	180°	The sugar is mahogany brown. It has to be poured onto an oiled baking sheet to cool quickly enough. (Photo 6) *Caramelized custard.*
	374°	190°	The caramel begins to smoke; it is too late to use it.

Brioche and Croissants

Yeast doughs have a very special place in the French baker's repertoire. They are essentially used for the rich butter rolls served plain with coffee for breakfast in France — as these recipes illustrate, however, they are extremely versatile doughs, and with some imagination can be turned into spectacular dessert presentations. *Ed.*

♛ ♛

23

Brioche Dough

This dough should be made the night before intended use. If preferred, it can be frozen and used at a later time. Brioche dough may be mixed with an electric mixer equipped with a dough hook, but it is best to knead small quantities by hand.

PREPARATION   30 minutes

RISING TIME   3½ to 5½ hours

RESTING TIME   12 hours

INGREDIENTS

For approximately 2 pounds 10 ounces (1,200 g) dough
1 pound (450 g) butter
1 cake (15 g) compressed baker's yeast
2 teaspoons warm water
2 teaspoons (15 g) salt
2 tablespoons (30 g) granulated sugar
1½ tablespoons milk
3¾ cups (500 g) flour
6 eggs

For approximately 1 pound 5 ounces (600 g) dough
½ pound (225 g) butter
½ cake (8 g) compressed baker's yeast
1 teaspoon warm water
1 teaspoon (8 g) salt
1 tablespoon (15 g) granulated sugar
2¼ teaspoons milk
1¾ cups (250 g) flour
3 eggs

For approximately 12½ ounces (360 g) dough
½ cup, generous (135 g), butter
⅓ cake (5 g) compressed baker's yeast
¾ teaspoon warm water
¾ teaspoon (5 g) salt
2 teaspoons (10 g) granulated sugar
1½ teaspoons milk
1 cup, generous (150 g), flour
2 eggs

3

4

UTENSILS   2 small bowls or glasses
1 large mixing bowl
Electric mixer with dough hook
Plastic scraper
Rolling pin
Plastic wrap or waxed paper

Note: This dough works best if made in large quantities. The following instructions are for making 2 pounds 10 ounces (1,200 g) of dough. The same method applies for making smaller amounts, but the amount of egg added at the various steps must be reduced according to the total number of eggs used.

Making the Dough: Take the butter out of the refrigerator 15 minutes before making the dough. Dissolve the yeast in the warm water. In another bowl, dissolve the salt and sugar in the milk. Never bring yeast into direct contact with salt or sugar.

Using an electric mixer: In the mixing bowl, place the salt-milk-sugar mixture. Add the flour, then add the yeast solution. Beat for 2 minutes at low speed, then all at once add 4 eggs and continue to beat until the dough is firm, homogenous, and smooth. Add the 2 remaining eggs one at a time, then beat at medium speed for 10 to 15 more minutes or until the dough is light and silky and no longer sticks to your fingers. Place the butter between 2 sheets of waxed paper or plastic wrap and tap it a few times with a rolling pin to flatten it. Break the butter into pieces the size of an egg. With the mixer on low speed, quickly add the butter to the dough—this should take no more than 2 minutes.

Kneading by hand: Have all the ingredients measured and ready for use. Place the flour on the table in a mound and make a well in the center. Put the yeast solution in the well and mix it with a little flour, then add 3 eggs. Incorporate about half the flour, then add the sugar-salt-milk mixture and 1 more egg, working with your fingers to mix all the ingredients together. When all the flour has been mixed in, knead the dough for 15 minutes, stretching it and slapping it back onto the table as you do so. When the time is up, add the remaining 2 eggs and keep working the dough until it becomes elastic and stretches easily without breaking. Now add the softened butter, prepared as described above for using an electric mixer, to ⅓ of the dough; then add the remaining dough, half of it at a time, using the plastic scraper to cut and mix the dough together (see photo 4, page 38). Try not to use your hands too much because the butter will melt too quickly.

5

Rising: Place the dough in a large bowl, cover the bowl with a cloth, and let it stand for 1½ to 2½ hours at room temperature. When the dough has risen to twice its original bulk, punch it down and stretch it twice (see photo 5, page 39). Let the dough rise again in the refrigerator for 2 or 3 hours until double its bulk again — it should be rounded on top like a ball. Punch the dough down as before, cover tightly, and keep it refrigerated overnight.

The next day, place the dough on a floured board and flatten it quickly by hand, then place it in the molds that will be used for baking (see photos 6–8).

To Freeze: The dough will keep for 1 month if wrapped tightly in plastic or aluminum foil. If you are making a large quantity, divide it into 2 or 3 pieces before freezing. Let the dough thaw for 24 hours in the refrigerator before using.

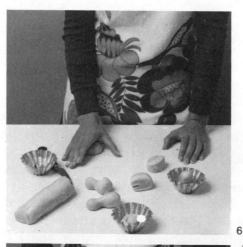

6

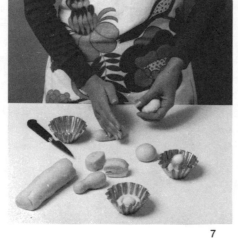

7

8

Individual Brioches

PREPARATION	15 minutes
RISING TIME	1 hour, 30 minutes
BAKING TIME	12 minutes
INGREDIENTS	*For 16 individual brioches* 1 pound (500 g) brioche dough (Recipe 23) 1 egg beaten with a pinch of salt
UTENSILS	16 individual brioche molds Pastry brush

Shaping the Dough: Prepare the brioche dough a day ahead.

On a lightly floured table, use your hands to roll the dough into a thick sausagelike shape. Divide it into 16 equal pieces. Dust the palms of your hands and the table with flour and roll each piece of dough into a ball. Don't press hard on the ball of dough while rolling it (see photo 6, page 40). Once a ball is formed, use the edge of your hand to dent the dough and form a smaller ball (or "head") for each brioche (see photo 7, page 40).

Butter each mold lightly with a pastry brush.

Place the dough in the molds with the small ball (or "head") on top. Use your fingers and gently press down the dough all around the bottom of the smaller ball or "head."

Let the dough rise for 1 hour, 30 minutes in a warm place.

Baking: Fifteen minutes before baking, preheat the oven to 450°F (230°C). Brush each brioche with a little beaten egg. Bake for about 12 minutes or until golden brown. Turn out while still warm.

25

Brioche Mousseline
(Photo page 36)

PREPARATION	15 minutes
RESTING TIME	2 hours
BAKING TIME	30 to 35 minutes
INGREDIENTS	*For a brioche serving 6 persons* 12½ ounces (360 g) brioche dough (Recipe 23) 1 beaten egg
UTENSILS	Mousseline mold (or 1-quart can) 4″ (10 cm) wide and 4¾″ (12 cm) tall Parchment paper or aluminum foil Scissors

Shaping the Dough: Prepare the brioche dough a day ahead.

Fold a large sheet of parchment paper or aluminum foil in half. Lightly butter the outside of the paper and use it to completely line the sides of the mold. The paper should be twice as wide as the mold is tall; this way the paper will not only line the mold but will form a cylinder that is taller than the mold itself. Butter the bottom of the mold and butter generously the interior surface of the paper.

Place the ball of dough at the bottom of the mold; press it down with your fist. Let it rise for 2 hours at room temperature or until the dough has risen up to ½″ (1 cm) from the edge of the mold.

Baking: Preheat the oven to 400°F (200°C).

Brush the dough with the beaten egg and cut a cross on the top with a pair of scissors. Bake for 30 to 35 minutes or until golden brown and firm to the touch. Turn out while still warm.

To Freeze: See Brioche Nanterre (Recipe 26).

26

Brioche Nanterre

(Photo page 36)

You can bake two brioches at the same time. One of them can be served right away and the other frozen for later use.

PREPARATION	15 minutes
RISING TIME	2 hours
BAKING TIME	35 minutes
INGREDIENTS	12½ ounces (360 g) brioche dough (Recipe 23) 1 beaten egg
UTENSILS	1 bread or loaf pan Pastry brush Parchment paper Scissors

Shaping the Dough: Prepare the brioche dough a day ahead.

Line the mold with buttered paper; the paper should be 1¼" (3 cm) higher than the mold.

Place the brioche dough on a lightly floured surface. Divide the dough into 6 equal parts. Shape each of the pieces into slightly oval balls.

Place the 6 balls of dough on the bottom of the mold. Let them rise for about 2 hours at room temperature or until they double in volume. They should then be all stuck together.

Baking: Preheat oven to 400°F (200°C).

Brush the dough with the beaten egg. With a pair of scissors that have been dipped into water, make a cross on the top of each mound of dough. Bake for 35 minutes or until golden brown and firm to the touch. Turn out while still warm.

To Freeze: The Brioche Nanterre should be frozen while still warm. To freeze, wrap in a plastic bag or aluminum foil. To thaw, let stand for 5 hours at room temperature or place in a 400°F (200°C) oven for 10 minutes, after letting it stand at room temperature for 1 hour.

27

Brioche Parisienne

(Photo page 36)

You can bake two of these large brioches at once and prepare a salpicon of fruit or a Brioche Polonaise with the extra.

PREPARATION	10 minutes
RISING TIME	1 hour, 30 minutes
BAKING TIME	35 minutes
INGREDIENTS	*For 1 large brioche* 12½ ounces (360 g) brioche dough (Recipe 23) 1 beaten egg
UTENSILS	Ribbed 7″ (18 cm) brioche mold Scissors Pastry brush

Shaping the Dough: Prepare the brioche dough a day ahead.

Place the dough on a lightly floured surface. Flour your hands and divide the dough into 2 balls, one large and one small (the small ball should be a little less than one third the size of the other). Roll the bigger ball of dough gently between your hands to make it smooth and round. Butter the mold and place the big ball of dough in it.

Roll the smaller ball of dough, shaping it like a pear. Make a depression in the top of the larger ball and place the narrow end of the smaller ball in the depression. Press lightly to make the two balls of dough stick together (see photo 17, page 50). Let the dough rise for an hour and a half at room temperature or until it has doubled in volume.

Baking: Preheat the oven to 400°F (200°C).

With scissors that have been dipped in water, cut slits on each side of the larger ball, then brush the dough with the beaten egg. Bake for 35 minutes or until golden brown. Turn out while still warm.

Note: Be careful not to let the beaten egg run down the sides of the mold; if it does, the brioche will stick to the mold.

To Store: This brioche will keep for up to 24 hours in the refrigerator if placed in a plastic bag or wrapped in aluminum foil.

To Freeze: Follow the instructions for Brioche Nanterre (Recipe 26).

Rolled Brioche with Candied Fruit

(Photo page 46)

This cake is an unusual mixture of brioche dough, candied fruits, rum, and pastry cream. It is delicious either as a dessert or at breakfast time.

PREPARATION	**45 minutes**
RISING TIME	**2 hours**
BAKING TIME	**35 minutes**
INGREDIENTS	*For 1 large brioche, serving 4 to 6 persons* ¼ cup (50 g) raisins 2 tablespoons rum 14 ounces (400 g) brioche dough (Recipe 23) 1⅓ cups (250 g) almond pastry cream (Recipe 5) *or* 1 cup (250 g) vanilla pastry cream (Recipe 2) ¼ cup (50 g) chopped candied fruit 1 egg, beaten ⅔ cup (1½ dl) dessert syrup (Recipe 11) *For the glaze* ⅔ cup (100 g) confectioners' sugar 2 tablespoons hot water 3 drops rum *or* apricot jam
UTENSILS	**Bowl** **Rolling pin** **Flexible blade-spatula** **Knife** **Cake pan 8″ (20 cm) round** **Pastry brush**

Assembling the Cake: Soak the raisins in the 2 tablespoons of rum for ½ hour. Take slightly more than a third of the chilled brioche dough (prepared a day in advance) and roll it out on a generously floured table until it is big enough to completely line the cake pan. Place it in the pan. Take one third of the pastry cream and spread it evenly over the bottom of the dough. Place the cake pan in the ice box while preparing the rest of the dough. On a generously floured table, roll out the remaining dough into a rectangle 10″ by 6″ (25 by 15 cm).

Spread the dough with the rest of the pastry cream, then sprinkle on the drained raisins and chopped candied fruit. Roll the dough into a 10″ (25 cm) long sausage and place in the refrigerator 15 minutes. Remove from the refrigerator and cut the roll of dough into 8 equal parts. Place these 8 pieces into the cake pan (see photo). There should be space between the rolls of dough and between the rolls and the sides of the cake pan. Put the cake pan in a warm place and leave to rise for about 2 hours, or until the dough has risen considerably and the rolls are touching.

Baking: Preheat the oven to 400°F (200°C).

Brush the top of the cake with the beaten egg, then bake for 35 minutes or until golden brown. If the top browns too quickly, cover it with aluminum foil.

When the cake is done, remove it from the oven and brush it with the dessert syrup (the cake will absorb all the syrup). Turn out while still warm, then let the cake cool. Decorate the surface of the cake with a white glaze made by mixing confectioners' sugar, rum, and water or make a shiny transparent glaze by painting the top of the cake with warm apricot jam.

To Store: This cake will stay fresh for 2 or 3 days in the refrigerator if it is kept covered.

♛ ♛

29

Kugelhopf Lenôtre

(Photo page 48)

This cake is prepared with a brioche dough, and it is richer than the Alsatian Kugelhopf, which follows (Recipe 30). It is a good idea to bake two at the same time and freeze one for later use.

PREPARATION	15 minutes
RISING TIME	2 hours
BAKING TIME	30 minutes
INGREDIENTS	*For 1 cake, serving 8 persons* 3 tablespoons rum ½ cup, scant (100 g), granulated sugar 6½ tablespoons (1 dl) water ½ cup (100 g) raisins 1 cup, generous (100 g), slivered almonds 12½ ounces (360 g) brioche dough (Recipe 23) 1 whole egg, beaten Confectioners' sugar (to decorate) Melted butter to brush the top of the cake

Small saucepan
              Pastry brush
              Kugelhopf mold 9½" (24 cm)
              Sugar dredger

Kugelhopf Lenôtre, Recipe 29

Shaping the Dough: Prepare a syrup by mixing the rum, sugar, and water in a saucepan. Bring this mixture to a boil, then remove from the heat. Soak the raisins for about 1 hour in this syrup (the syrup can be kept for several weeks in the refrigerator if placed in a tightly sealed container).

Butter the mold and sprinkle all over with slivered almonds. On a lightly floured board, roll the chilled brioche dough into a long rectangle. Drain the raisins, place them on top of the dough and roll the dough tightly in a long roll; bring the ends together to form a circle and stick them together with some beaten egg. Place the dough in the mold; let the dough rise at a temperature of about 80°F (25°C) for 2 hours or until the dough fills ¾ of the mold.

Baking: Preheat the oven to 400°F (200°C). Bake the cake for 30 minutes; check the color after 20 minutes. If the Kugelhopf is already brown on top, finish the baking after covering it with aluminum foil. To find out if the Kugelhopf is done, insert a knife; if the blade comes out dry, it is cooked. Turn out the Kugelhopf while it is still warm. Brush the surface of the cake with melted butter and dust with confectioners' sugar just before serving.

To Freeze: You can freeze the Kugelhopf while it is still lukewarm, but do not brush on the butter or dust with confectioners' sugar. When you take the cake out of the freezer, let it thaw for 2 hours at room temperature and then bake at 325°F (150°C) for 10 minutes to warm the cake. Brush the surface of the cake as indicated above and serve.

♟ ♟

30

Alsatian Kugelhopf

PREPARATION	**15 minutes**
RESTING TIME	**2 hours**
BAKING TIME	**30 minutes**
INGREDIENTS	*For 1 cake, serving 8 persons*
	1 cake (15 g) compressed baker's yeast
	2 teaspoons warm water
	1 teaspoon (7 g) salt
	¼ cup (60 g) granulated sugar
	6½ tablespoons (1 dl) milk
	3¾ cups (500 g) flour
	4 whole eggs
	¾ cup, generous (200 g), butter

Preparing the Dough: Using the ingredients listed here, make a dough following the instructions given for the brioche dough (Recipe 23). This dough will not be as rich as the brioche dough given in Recipe 23. Use it instead of brioche dough to make a Kugelhopf, following the instructions given in the previous recipe.

Brioche Filled with Fruit Salad

If Bavarian cream and the chocolate mousse are too rich for your taste, a brioche can be filled with fresh fruit salad.

PREPARATION	15 minutes
RESTING TIME	2 to 3 hours
INGREDIENTS	*For 8 servings* 1 brioche prepared a day ahead (Recipe 25 or 27) 2 cups, generous (300 g), tropical fruit salad (Recipe 96) Cold butter
UTENSILS	Serrated knife

Assembling the Brioche: Prepare the fresh fruit salad two or three hours ahead of time, using whatever fruit is in season. For instance, fruit salad in the wintertime: oranges, bananas, apples, pears, prunes, and raisins. Fruit salad in the summertime: strawberries, raspberries, gooseberries, peaches, and very ripe apricots. Exotic fruit salad: lichees, mangoes, guavas, mangosteens (this is a tropical fruit from Malaysia). Sugar the fruit salad to your taste and pour a little lemon juice over it to bring out the flavor of the fruit (it will also prevent the fruit from turning black). Refrigerate.

Hollow out the brioche. Close the bottom hole with a dab of cold butter. Just before serving, fill the brioche with the fruit salad. If you have extra fruit salad, serve it in a bowl alongside the brioche.

Note: Fruit salad will taste and look better when a fruit sauce is poured over it. For example, in winter, use a pear sauce; in the summer, use a raspberry or an apricot sauce.

Brioche Polonaise

This is another inventive dessert with a brioche as its main ingredient.

PREPARATION	45 minutes
BAKING TIME	10 minutes
INGREDIENTS	*For 8 servings*
	1 Parisian brioche(Recipe 27)
	$^2/_3$ cup ($1^1/_2$ dl) rum-flavored dessert syrup (Recipe 11)
	$1^3/_4$ cups, generous (450 g), vanilla pastry cream (Recipe 2) flavored with $^1/_2$ teaspoon rum
	$^1/_2$ cup (100 g) chopped candied fruit
	$^1/_3$ cup (50 g) whole candied cherries
	For the Italian meringue
	4 egg whites = $^2/_3$ cup (120 g)
	1 cup, generous (250 g), granulated sugar
	3 tablespoons water
	For the decoration
	Slivered almonds
	Confectioners' sugar
UTENSILS	1 cake pan (wider than the brioche)
	Spatula
	Pastry brush
	Mixing bowl
	Electric mixer
	Sugar dredger
	Thermometer [optional]

Preparing the Brioche: Cut off the top of the brioche and cut the brioche in four equal slices horizontally. (You can lightly toast each slice [optional].)

Brush the bottom slice of the brioche with the syrup. Place that slice on the bottom of the cake pan. Spread a layer of pastry cream on this first slice, then some chopped candied fruit and candied cherries, then place another slice of brioche on top, brush with syrup, and cover as described above. Continue in this way with all the layers. Then, replace the top of the brioche (brush the inside of the top with syrup before putting it into place).

Making the Meringue: To prepare the Italian meringue, beat the egg whites until very stiff, adding 2 teaspoons of sugar halfway through. Mix the remaining sugar with the water, boil until it reaches the hard ball stage—248°F (120°C) —on the candy thermometer or until one drop of sugar holds its shape when dropped into a glass of cold water. Still beating at low speed, pour the boiling sugar into the egg whites, between the beaters and the sides of the mixing bowl. Keep on beating at low speed until the mixture is cool (about 5 minutes).

Baking: Preheat the oven to 475°F (240°C).

Using a spatula, completely cover the brioche with a ½" (1 cm) layer of meringue. Sprinkle with slivered almonds and confectioners' sugar.

Bake for about 10 minutes or until the meringue hardens and begins to brown. Turn off the oven after 5 minutes if the meringue browns too quickly, but leave the brioche for 5 minutes more in the oven to finish cooking.

Note: You can replace the rum by Kirsch when making the dessert syrup and pastry cream.

♛ ♛

33

Raisin Buns

These buns are found in every Parisian bakery. The brioche dough used in making them is best prepared a day ahead of time.

PREPARATION   45 minutes

RESTING TIME   1 hour

BAKING TIME   10 minutes

INGREDIENTS   *For 10 individual buns*
¼ cup (50 g) raisins
1 cup (¼ l) boiling water
3 tablespoons (½ dl) rum
9 ounces (250 g) brioche dough (Recipe 23)
½ cup (100 g) almond pastry cream (Recipe 5) *or*
    vanilla pastry cream (Recipe 2)
1 egg, beaten

For the icing
⅔ cup (100 g) confectioners' sugar
3 drops rum
2 tablespoons water *or*
3 tablespoons apricot jam

UTENSILS

Small mixing bowl
Rolling pin
Pastry brush
Parchment paper
Baking sheet

Shaping the Buns: Soak the raisins in the boiling water for 15 minutes. Drain, then soak them in the rum while you roll out the dough. On a lightly floured board, roll the brioche dough into a rectangle 10″ by 6″ (25 cm by 15 cm). Cover the dough with the pastry cream of your choice, then drain the raisins and place them on top of the cream. Roll the dough tightly into a 10″ (25 cm) long roll. Place in the refrigerator for 30 minutes, then cut into 10 equal pieces (see photo, page 2). Place each piece of dough on a lightly buttered baking sheet (or a baking sheet lined with parchment paper), and let them rise for about 1 hour.

Baking: Preheat the oven to 425°F (220°C).
   Brush the top of the buns with beaten egg. Bake the buns for 10 minutes. Remove the baking sheet from the oven and let the buns cool. While they are still warm, brush them either with an icing made by mixing confectioners' sugar, rum, and water or with a glaze made by melting a little apricot jam.

34

Croissants

(Photo page 58)

PREPARATION   **20 minutes**

RESTING TIME   **7 hours minimum**

BAKING TIME   **15 minutes per baking sheet**

For approximately 2 pounds 3 ounces (1 kg) dough; sufficient for 30 Croissants
1 cake (18 g) compressed baker's yeast
1½ tablespoons warm water
3½ tablespoons (50 g) granulated sugar
2 teaspoons (15 g) salt
1½ tablespoons milk
3 tablespoons (40 g) butter
½ cup (125 ml) water
½ cup (125 ml) milk
3¾ cups (500 g) flour
1¼ cups, scant (260 g), butter
1 beaten egg (for glazing)

For approximately 1 pound 1½ ounces (500 g) dough; sufficient for 15 Croissants
½ cake (9 g) compressed baker's yeast
2¼ teaspoons warm water
5 teaspoons (25 g) granulated sugar
1 teaspoon (8 g) salt
2¼ teaspoons milk
1½ tablespoons (20 g) butter
¼ cup (65 ml) water
¼ cup (65 ml) milk
1¾ cups (250 g) flour
½ cup, generous (130 g), butter
½ beaten egg (for glazing)

UTENSILS

2 small mixing bowls
1 large mixing bowl
Small saucepan
Shallow baking dish
Electric mixer
2 baking sheets
Pastry brush

Making the Dough: Dissolve the yeast in the warm water. In another bowl, mix the sugar and the salt with 2 tablespoons of milk. When this is done, melt 3 tablespoons (40 g) butter in a small saucepan, then add ½ cup (125 ml) water and ½ cup (125 ml) milk and heat until the mixture is lukewarm. Then place the flour in the large mixing bowl, and with the mixer set at a low speed, add the sugar-milk mixture to the flour. Increase the speed of the mixer slightly and add the butter-milk mixture, beat for about a minute and add the dissolved yeast. The dough will be very light and lukewarm. Cover the bowl with a towel and let it rise in a warm place (80°F-25°C) for about 1 hour or until the dough has doubled in volume. Then place the dough in a lightly floured shallow baking dish, spreading it out evenly. Cover the dough and chill it in the refrigerator for 2 to 3 hours.

Half an hour before you intend to roll out the dough, remove the butter from the refrigerator and cut it in two. Leave one half at room temperature to soften. Put the remaining half back in the refrigerator.

Rolling out and Shaping the Dough: Place the dough on a lightly floured surface and roll it into a rectangle. Cover ⅔ of the dough with the softened half of the butter, which has been broken into small pieces. Fold the rectangle in thirds, starting with the side that was not buttered, then roll out the dough once and fold in thirds as for flaky pastry (see photo 10, page 62 and instructions for flaky pastry, Recipes 36 and 37). Return the dough to the refrigerator and let it stand, covered, for at least 2 hours, or for best results, overnight.

Roll out the dough again, softening and adding the remaining butter as described above. After folding in thirds, roll the dough in a rectangle 8″ by 10″ (20 by 25 cm). Return the dough to the refrigerator, covered, for 1 hour.

Roll the dough out until it is very thin ($1/16$″ [3 mm] thick) and forms a rectangle 36″ by 12″ (90 by 30 cm), then cut the rectangle in two, lengthwise. Cut each band of dough into 15 triangles, and then roll each triangle into a sausage shape, rolling from the base toward the point of each triangle. Bend the edges of each little roll of dough inward to make them crescent-shaped.

Place the crescent-shaped rolls on buttered baking sheets, leaving spaces between them. Brush them with beaten egg, using a pastry brush. This will keep the rolls from drying out as they rise. Set the sheets in a warm place and allow the croissants to rise for 2 hours, or until they double in size.

Baking: Preheat the oven to 400°F (200°C).

Brush the croissants once more with beaten egg and bake for 15 minutes, or until golden brown. Watch the color because not all the croissants will bake at the same rate. If you wish to bake the entire recipe of 30 croissants, it would be better to bake them in 2 batches.

To Freeze: After baking, allow the croissants to cool for a few minutes. While still warm, put them on a plate, then place the plate in the freezer to quick-freeze the croissants. As soon as they are hard, put them in a plastic bag and return to the freezer.

When you want to eat them, preheat the oven to 475°F (250°C) for 15 minutes, then remove the croissants from the freezer and bake them for exactly 5 minutes to heat them through.

Once frozen, the croissants will stay good for 2 weeks.

♕ ♕

Chocolate Rolls

(Photo page 58)

These rolls are made with the same dough as Croissants (Recipe 34). They are a favorite with schoolchildren in France who usually buy them around five in the afternoon to eat as a snack on their way home from school.

PREPARATION	10 minutes
RESTING TIME	1 hour
BAKING TIME	18 minutes per sheet
INGREDIENTS	*For 15 rolls* 1 pound 1½ ounces (500 g) Croissant dough (Recipe 34) 15 small, semi-sweet chocolate bars, ⅓ ounces (10 g) each *or* 5 ounces (150 g) semi-sweet chocolate chips 1 egg, beaten
UTENSILS	Rolling pin Knife Waxed paper Pastry brush Baking sheet

Assembling the Rolls: Follow the recipe given for preparing Croissants, but when you roll this dough for the second time before cutting it, roll it into a rectangle 6″ by 35″ (15 cm by 90 cm). Then cut the dough into 15 smaller rectangles, 6″ by 2⅜″ (15 cm by 6 cm). Place a chocolate bar across each rectangle, about 1½″ (4 cm) from one end and roll the dough around the chocolate (see photo, page 58). Place these small rolls on a well-buttered baking sheet and cover with waxed paper. Let the rolls rise at room temperature for 1 hour.

Baking: Preheat the oven to 475°F (250°C).
   Remove the waxed paper and brush the rolls with beaten egg; bake for 3 minutes at 475°F (250°C), then lower the temperature to 400°F (200°C) and continue baking for 15 minutes longer. Watch the color because the Chocolate Rolls will not all bake at the same rate. Bake until golden brown.

Note: If using chocolate chips, sprinkle them in a thin line across each rectangle of dough, then roll the dough around the line of chips as if they were a chocolate bar.

Flaky Pastries

Flaky pastry is one of the great French contributions to gastronomy. It is the lightest of pastries and one of the richest as well. Making flaky pastry is no simple task for the beginner, but once you have mastered the technique so carefully described here, a new realm of desserts will be opened to you. *Ed.*

♙ ♙ ♙

36

Classic Flaky Pastry

Flaky pastry is made by wrapping cold butter inside cold dough, then rolling it out and folding it several times. This produces a very flaky dough, made up of many layers, which will rise to several times its original height when baked. It is difficult to make well, since it demands a great deal of care and patience, but the photographs will make the various steps easier to follow.

PREPARATION   30 minutes

RESTING TIME   5 hours

INGREDIENTS   *For approximately 2 pounds 14 ounces (1,300 g) dough*
2 teaspoons (15 g) salt
1 cup (¼ l) water
3¾ cups (500 g) flour
5 tablespoons (75 g) softened butter
2¼ cups (500 g) cold butter

For approximately 1 pound 7 ounces (650 g) dough
1 teaspoon (8 g) salt
½ cup (12.5 cl) water
1¾ cups (250 g) flour
2½ tablespoons (38 g) softened butter
1 cup, generous (250 g), cold butter

For approximately 9 ounces (250 g) dough
½ teaspoon, scant (3 g), salt
3 tablespoons (5 cl) water
¾ cup (100 g) flour
1 tablespoon (15 g) softened butter
6½ tablespoons (100 g) cold butter
(for these small quantities, mix the dough by hand)

UTENSILS

Small bowl or glass
Large mixing bowl
Electric mixer with dough hook
Plastic scraper
Plastic wrap or waxed paper
Cardboard rulers

Making the Dough: In a small bowl or glass, dissolve the salt in the water. In the mixing bowl, place the flour and the softened butter. Beat for 30 seconds at low speed, then add the salt water. If necessary, finish mixing the dough by hand, cutting it with the plastic scraper. The butter should be completely incorporated. Form a ball with the dough and cut the top crosswise with a knife. Refrigerate covered for 2 hours.

Rolling out the Dough: Place the cold butter between 2 sheets of waxed paper or plastic wrap and tap it several times with a rolling pin in order to flatten it slightly and make it more pliable. Roll the dough into a square on a floured surface, place the butter in the center, and fold in the sides (see photo 9). The butter should be completely enclosed inside the dough.

Place the folded dough so that the line of the last fold is perpendicular to you. Lightly flour the surface of the dough and the rolling pin. If necessary, sprinkle a little more flour on the rolling surface as well.

9

10

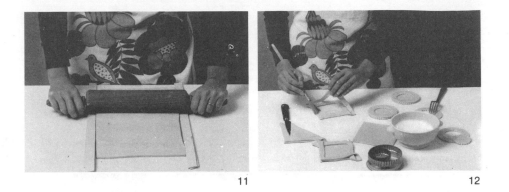

11   12

Roll the dough out into a long rectangle slightly more than ¼ inch thick, checking frequently to make sure the dough is not sticking to the table. Reflour the table and rolling pin when necessary, but do so as lightly as possible each time. When the desired thickness is reached, fold the dough into thirds.

Give the dough ¼ turn so the line of the fold is again perpendicular to you. You should **never roll across this fold, but always roll along it (see photo 10, page 62). Roll the dough out a second time, and fold it in thirds once more. Refrigerate the dough, well covered, for 1 hour.**

Give the dough 2 more turns (i.e., roll and fold it 2 more times). Refrigerate again for 1 hour. Just before using the dough, whether frozen or just refrigerated, give it 2 more turns and chill it for 1 hour in the refrigerator before rolling it into the shape asked for in any specific recipe.

Note: To roll the dough evenly, cut some cardboard rulers, 10″ long (25 cm). Place several of these rulers on top of each other until you reach the thickness you want the dough to be. The rulers will serve as a frame. You can then roll the dough 1/16″ (2 mm) or 1/8″ (3 mm), etc., to make small tarts (see photo 12), or other desserts, depending on the thickness the recipe calls for.

If the butter breaks through the dough, flour the broken places generously; also flour the rolling pin or table, depending upon whether the butter broke through the top or bottom. Continue rolling gently, until approximately the correct thickness, fold in thirds and refrigerate for 1 hour before continuing. Then proceed as directed, rolling the dough as gently and quickly as possible.

To Store: The dough will keep 3 to 4 days in the refrigerator if wrapped tightly in aluminum foil or plastic. After this time, however, it will begin to discolor and will eventually turn black.

To Freeze: Move the dough from the freezer to the refrigerator 24 hours before you intend to use it.

Quick Flaky Pastry

This method of making flaky pastry differs slightly from the classic method, cutting the time needed to make it almost in half. However, it does not keep as well as classic flaky pastry, so it is best to use it the day it is made.

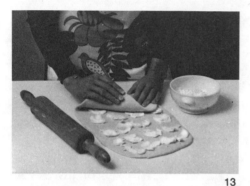

13   14

PREPARATION	20 minutes
RESTING TIME	3 hours
INGREDIENTS	*For approximately 2 pounds 3 ounces (1 kg) dough* 3¾ cups (500 g) flour ¾ cup, generous (200 g), softened butter 2 teaspoons (15 g) salt ¾ cup (2 dl) water ¾ cup, generous (200 g), cold butter *For approximately 1 pound 7 ounces (650 g) dough* 2¼ cups (325 g) flour ⅔ cup, scant (130 g), softened butter 1½ teaspoons (10 g) salt ½ cup (1.25 dl) water ⅔ cup, scant (130 g), cold butter *For approximately 9 ounces (250 g) dough* 1 cup, scant (125 g), flour

3 tablespoons (50 g) softened butter
½ teaspoon (4 g) salt
3 tablespoons (5 cl) water
3 tablespoons (50 g) cold butter
(for these small quantities, mix the dough by hand)

UTENSILS

1 large mixing bowl
1 medium-sized bowl
Electric mixer with dough hook
Plastic scraper
Rolling pin
Plastic wrap or waxed paper
Cardboard rulers

Making the Dough: In the mixing bowl, place the flour and softened butter, broken into pieces. Mix at low speed for 30 seconds, then add the salt and water. Finish kneading the dough by hand if necessary, using the scraper to completely incorporate the butter. Form a ball with the dough. Place the dough in the second bowl and cover it with a plate or a floured cloth. Let it stand for 1 hour in the refrigerator.

Rolling out the Dough: Place the butter between 2 sheets of waxed paper or plastic wrap and tap it several times with the rolling pin to make it more pliable.

Lightly flour the dough and the rolling surface. Roll the dough out into a rectangle about ¼ inch thick. Break the butter into pieces, and cover ⅔ of the dough with them. Fold the dough into thirds, beginning with the third which was not covered with butter (see photo 13, page 64).

Turn the dough so that the line of the fold is perpendicular to you. Roll it out into a rectangle again—this time slightly less than ½ inch thick. Check frequently to be sure the dough does not stick to the table. Reflour the table and the dough whenever necessary, but as lightly as possible. Fold the dough in fourths; i.e., fold the ends until they touch in the middle, then fold the dough in half (see photo 14, page 64).

Give the dough a ¼ turn so the folded edge is perpendicular to you. Roll it out again and fold it in fourths again. At this stage, the dough is said to have been given 2 double turns. Cover it well and chill it for 1 hour in the refrigerator.

If you don't intend to use all of the dough right away, it is best to freeze what is left over because it cannot be stored for more than a day in the refrigerator.

To Freeze: Wrap the dough tightly in aluminum foil or plastic wrap before freezing. Before using the dough, let it defrost for 24 hours in the refrigerator.

Using the Dough: Whether the dough has been frozen or simply chilled as described above, it should be given 2 more turns as described in Recipe 36 for Classic Flaky Pastry and set to chill for one hour more before being rolled out into the shape required for any specific recipe.

38

Pithiviers

This is a dessert made from flaky pastry and almond cream. It was once a specialty of the town of Pithiviers but is now prepared all over France.

PREPARATION	20 minutes
RESTING TIME	30 minutes
BAKING TIME	45 minutes to an hour

INGREDIENTS	*For 1 cake, serving 8 persons*
	2 cups, generous (400 g), almond pastry
	    cream (Recipe 5)
	1 pound 5 ounces (600 g) classic *or* quick flaky pastry
	    dough (Recipe 36 or 37)
	1 egg, beaten
	1½ tablespoons (15 g) confectioners' sugar

UTENSILS	Rolling pin Saucer Pastry brush Knife Baking sheet Sugar dredger

Assembling the Cake: Preheat the oven to 475°F (245°C).

Divide the dough into two equal parts. On a lightly floured board, roll each piece of dough into a circle. To roll the dough into a perfect circle, roll it first into a small square barely larger than a saucer, place the saucer upside down on the dough and cut around it with a knife. Place this excess dough in the center of the circle and continue rolling the dough until it forms a large circle 10½" (26 cm) wide and ⅛" (3 mm) thick. Roll out the other piece of dough, so you will have two circles of dough the same size and thickness.

Place one circle on the baking sheet and brush a ½" (1 cm) band of beaten egg around the rim of the circle; don't get any egg on the edge of the dough. Place the almond pastry cream in the center of this circle of dough and spread it to within about 1" (3 cm) of the edge. Cover this circle of dough with the remaining circle and press down the edges so that they will stick together. Refrigerate the cake for 30 minutes.

Baking: Brush the top of the cake with the remaining beaten egg. Using the point of the knife, make a decorative design, drawing semi-circles in a spiral shape, starting from the center of the cake out to the edges (see photo page **66**). Bake the cake at 475°F (245°C). When the Pithiviers has risen (after about 15 minutes), lower the heat to 400°F (200°C). Continue baking for 30 to 40 minutes more. Ten minutes before the cake is done, sprinkle the top with confectioners' sugar. Serve the cake warm.

♛ ♛

39

Apple Dartois

PREPARATION	15 minutes
BAKING TIME	30 minutes
INGREDIENTS	*For 8 servings* 12 ounces (350 g) apples, peeled, cored, and diced 1 cup, generous (300 g), apple sauce ¾ teaspoon vanilla powder *or* extract 3 tablespoons (40 g) granulated sugar 1 pound 1½ ounces (500 g) classic *or* quick flaky pastry dough (Recipe 36 or 37) 1 egg, beaten
UTENSILS	Mixing bowl Baking sheet Rolling pin Pastry brush Fork

Assembling the Cake: Preheat the oven to 475°F (240°C).

In a bowl, mix the diced apples, apple sauce, vanilla powder, and sugar. Divide the dough into 2 equal parts, roll each piece into a ¹/₁₆″ (2 mm) thick

rectangle. Both rectangles should be the same size and shape. Place the first rectangle on a baking sheet and prick with a fork. Wet with a pastry brush 1¼" (3 cm) all around the edges, then spread the apple filling evenly over the surface without touching the wet border.

Prick the second rectangle of dough, then lay it on top of the first one, pressing the edges together to seal them.

Baking: Brush the entire surface with a beaten egg and, with a knife, draw lines to form a diamond-shaped pattern on the top of the cake. Bake in a 475°F (240°C) oven for 5 minutes, reduce the heat to 425°F (220°C), and bake for 25 minutes more.

40

Eleanor's Apple Tart

This tart is made with flaky pastry topped with apples. Some people like serving a bowl of heavy cream with the tart, but it is delicious alone as well.

PREPARATION	15 minutes
BAKING TIME	20 minutes
INGREDIENTS	*For 6 servings, or 3 tarts 7″ (18 cm) wide* 7 ounces (200 g) flaky pastry dough (Recipe 36 or 37) 6 tablespoons (100 g) apple sauce 5 cooking apples, peeled, cored, quartered Confectioners sugar to sprinkle on tarts 4 tablespoons (60 g) butter 3 tablespoons crème fraîche *or* heavy cream [optional]
UTENSILS	Rolling pin Baking sheet Sugar dredger

Baking: Preheat the oven to 450°F (240°C).

Roll out the flaky pastry until it is ⅛″ (3 mm) thick. Cut the dough into three circles, placing the excess dough in the center of each circle. Roll out each circle until it is 7″ (18 cm) wide, then place the three circles on a baking sheet.

In the center of each circle of dough, place a thin layer (2 tablespoons) of apple sauce (leave a border 1½″ wide uncovered around the edges).

Cut the quartered apples in half and place these pieces of apple in a circle on top of the apple sauce on top of each tart (see photo). Sprinkle each tart generously with confectioners' sugar and place small dabs of butter on top of the sugar.

Bake the tarts in a 450°F (240°C) oven for about 20 minutes. Five minutes before the end of baking, sprinkle each tart again with confectioners' sugar to glaze the fruit. Serve while warm, either as is or with a tablespoon of cream on each tart.

41

Tarte Tatin

Caramelized apples characterize this tart which is cooked "upside down" with a flaky pie crust.

PREPARATION	10 minutes
COOKING TIME	20 minutes
BAKING TIME	25 minutes
INGREDIENTS	*For 8 servings* 6¼ ounces (180 g) flaky pastry dough (Recipe 36 or 37) ½ cup (120 g) butter 1¼ cups, scant (270 g), granulated sugar 2¾ pounds (1.250 kg) tart cooking apples, peeled, cored, and halved
UTENSILS	Cake pan or preferably a round cast-iron enameled dish 9½″ (24 cm) wide and 2″ (5 cm) high Fork Rolling pin

Assembling the Tart: On a floured table, roll out the dough ¹/₁₆″ (2 mm) thick into a 10″ (26 cm) circle. Place the dough on a plate and prick it with a fork. Refrigerate, while you prepare the apples.

Preheat the oven to 400°F (200°C).

In the pie pan or dish, melt the butter and the sugar on top of the stove, then place the apples in the dish very close together. Continue cooking very slowly until the sugar begins to caramelize. This should take about 20 minutes and the apples should soften considerably. The caramel should be very light in color.

Baking: Put the dish in the oven for 5 minutes, then cover the apples with the rolled out flaky dough. Raise the oven temperature to 450°F (240°C) and continue baking for 20 minutes or until the pie crust looks done.

Once cooked, turn the dish over on a serving platter. Serve the tart warm.

42

Pineapple Tartlets

PREPARATION | 45 minutes

BAKING TIME | 20 minutes

INGREDIENTS

For 10 pineapple tartlets
12 ounces (350 g) flaky pastry dough (Recipe 36 or 37)
1 cup (250 g) vanilla pastry cream (Recipe 2), flavored with
   2 teaspoons rum
10 slices canned pineapple, drained
5 large candied cherries
⅓ cup (100 g) apricot jam, warm

UTENSILS

Knife
Rolling pin
Fork
Pastry brush
Baking sheet

Preparing the Tartlets: Preheat the oven to 425°F (220°C).

On a lightly floured table, roll out the flaky pastry very thin. To prepare square tartlets, cut the dough into squares 3″ (8 cm) on each side. Fold each square in half (forming a triangle) and cut around the two short sides making a band ½″ (1 cm) wide—but do not detach this band or cut all the way to the end. Open the square, fold over the cut ends, crossing each one to the opposite side (see photo, page 74 and photo 12, page 63). Prick the bottom of each tartlet with a fork and lightly wet the edges so that the border will stick to the bottom. Place the unfilled tartlets on a baking sheet and bake in a 425°F (220°C) oven for 20 minutes or until golden brown, then remove and allow to cool.

Filling and Decorating: The baked and cooled tartlets are filled with a layer of rum-flavored pastry cream, then decorated with the pineapple. Place half a candied cherry on each tartlet and brush with the apricot jam to glaze.

Serve as soon as possible since flaky pastry gets soggy after being filled.

43

Palmiers

PREPARATION	15 minutes
RESTING TIME	10 minutes
BAKING TIME	10 minutes per sheet
INGREDIENTS	*For 60 palmiers* 7 ounces (200 g) classic flaky pastry dough (Recipe 36) ½ cup, generous (80 g), confectioners' sugar, plus 1 teaspoon powdered vanilla 1 teaspoon powdered vanilla
UTENSILS	Rolling pin Knife Parchment paper [optional] 2 baking sheets Pastry brush

Shaping the Dough: On a table, sprinkled heavily with confectioners' sugar, give the dough the last 2 turns; then freeze for 5 minutes. Roll the dough out again in the confectioners' sugar into 2 strips 6″ by 12″ (15 × 30 cm). Moisten the dough lightly with a damp pastry brush. Fold in the sides of the dough until they touch in the center (fold lengthwise). Fold again lengthwise, this time in half, pressing down lightly. The dough will now be 4 layers thick (see photo, page 76). Place these strips in the freezer for 3 to 5 minutes. When the dough has hardened, slice each strip into ¼″ (½ cm) thick slices. Place each slice on a buttered or parchment paper-lined baking sheet. Do not place the palmiers too close to one another as they spread while baking.

Baking: Preheat the oven to 400°F (200°C). Bake one sheet at a time; leave the remaining dough in the freezer until ready to use. Bake in a 400°F (200°C) oven for 10 minutes, then remove and allow to cool. Do not place the palmiers on top of each other until they are completely cold or else they will stick together.

To Store: Palmiers will keep 8 days in a tightly sealed container.

44

Glazed Match Sticks

(Photo page 76)

PREPARATION	15 minutes
BAKING TIME	10 minutes
INGREDIENTS	*For 36 pastries* 1 cup (150 g) confectioners' sugar 1 egg white 3 drops lemon juice 7 ounces (200 g) classic flaky pastry dough (Recipe 36)
UTENSILS	Spoon Bowl Knife Rolling pin 4 tartlet rings ¾" (2 cm) high Cake rack Ruler Baking sheet

Making the Icing: Make an icing by beating the confectioners' sugar with the egg white for about 2 minutes, using a spoon, until the mixture is light and homogenous. Then stir in the lemon.

Baking: Preheat the oven to 400°F (200°C). On a lightly floured table, roll out the dough into a rectangle 16" by 8" (40 × 20 cm). Using a ruler and a knife, cut the dough in three 16" (40 cm) long pieces. Fold two of these pieces and refrigerate while preparing the third piece of dough. Place this piece of dough on a slightly damp baking sheet. Cover the dough with the icing (spreading it evenly about ¹/₁₆" [1.5mm] thick). Cut the dough into about 12 strips (using a damp knife). Ice and cut the two remaining pieces of dough the same way. Place all the sticks on the same baking sheet. Before baking, place on each corner of the baking sheet a small ¾" (2 cm) high tartlet ring on top of which you place a cake rack so that the dough will rise evenly and each pastry will be the same height.

Bake in a 400°F (200°C) oven for 10 minutes, keeping the oven door ajar with a spoon. Bake until golden brown. During the baking, the sticks shrink a little in width and will detach themselves from each other. If you used too much icing and the pastry sticks together, cut the sticks apart with a knife while they are baking.

To Store: These little pastries will keep 10 days in a tightly closed container, but be sure the sticks are completely cool before storing them.

45

Sacristains

15 minutes

30 minutes per sheet

For 80 cookies
1 pound (450 g) classic flaky pastry dough (Recipe 36) *or*
    quick flaky pastry dough (Recipe 37)
1 cup, generous (160 g), broken rock candy
1 cup (160 g) chopped almonds
1 egg, beaten

Pastry brush
Rolling pin
Knife
2 baking sheets

Shaping the Dough: Work quickly. On a lightly floured table, roll out the cold dough into a rectangle 5½″ × 15″ (14 × 40 cm), ¹/₁₆″ (2 mm) thick. Cut the dough lengthwise into 2 equal strips. Fold one of the strips in half and refrigerate. Brush the other strip with a little beaten egg. Sprinkle with ¼ of the rock candy and ¼ of the chopped almonds. Press the almonds and sugar into the dough lightly with a rolling pin. Turn the dough upside down and brush the other side with a little beaten egg, then sprinkle with chopped almonds and sugar as just described.

Cut this strip of dough into rectangles ¾″ by 2¾″ (2 cm × 7 cm); twist each rectangle slightly to form the cookies (see photo, page 76).

Baking: Preheat the oven to 400°F (200°C). Place the cookies on a baking sheet (about 40 per sheet). Bake for 10 minutes in a 400°F (200°C) oven, then lower the heat to 325°F (160°C) and bake for another 20 minutes. The cookies will puff up and shorten during baking. Meanwhile, remove the second strip of dough from the refrigerator and prepare and bake as described above.

To Store: In a tightly sealed container, these cookies will keep for 6 days.

Cream Puff Pastries

In addition to cream puffs, cream puff pastry is the basic dough for the ring shaped Paris-Brest and the cream-filled St. Honoré cakes. Not only one of the easiest doughs to make, it is one of the easiest to shape as well. *Ed.*

46

Cream Puff Pastry (Pâte à Chou)

Do not work this dough too long or else the puffs will not rise correctly.

PREPARATION	15 minutes
BAKING TIME	20 to 30 minutes per baking sheet
INGREDIENTS	*For approximately 1⅓ cups (600 g) dough* 4-5 eggs = 1 cup (¼ l), beaten 1 cup (¼ l) mixture of half milk, half water ¾ teaspoon (5 g) salt 1 teaspoon (5 g) granulated sugar 7½ tablespoons (110 g) butter 1 cup (140 g) flour Confectioners' sugar
	For approximately ⅔ cup (300 g) dough 2-3 eggs = ½ cup (12.5 cl), beaten ½ cup (12.5 cl) mixture of half milk, half water ¼ teaspoon, generous (2.5 g), salt ½ teaspoon (2.5 g) granulated sugar 3½ tablespoons (55 g) butter ½ cup (70 g) flour Confectioners' sugar

For approximately ½ cup, scant (200 g), dough
1-2 eggs = ⅓ cup (8 cl), beaten
⅓ cup (8 cl) mixture of half milk, half water
¼ teaspoon (1.5 g) salt
¼ teaspoon, generous (1.5 g) granulated sugar
2 tablespoons (35 g) butter
⅓ cup (45 g) flour
Confectioners' sugar

UTENSILS

Large, thick-bottomed saucepan
Mixing bowl, warmed
Wooden spoon
Wire whisk
Pastry bag with ⅝" (1.5 cm) or ½" (1 cm) nozzle
Sugar dredger
Baking sheets, as needed

Making the Dough: Preheat oven to 425°F (220°C). Measure the eggs, since their volume can be more or less than the actual amount required by the recipe.

Place the water-milk mixture in the saucepan and add the salt, sugar, and butter. Bring slowly to a boil, then remove from the heat and add all the flour at one time. Beat the dough vigorously with a wooden spoon, replace the saucepan on the heat, and beat the dough for 1 minute or until it comes away from the sides of the pan and no longer sticks to the spoon. Transfer the dough to a warmed mixing bowl. Add a third of the beaten egg, beating the dough all the while with the spoon. When the egg is mixed in, add half the remaining egg, still beating the dough; finally, add the remaining egg and continue to beat until the dough is smooth.

Baking: Fill the pastry bag with the dough. Butter and flour the baking sheets or line them with waxed paper, sticking each corner of the paper to the sheet with some of the dough. Make 1½" (4 cm) rounds or, if you are experienced, make long eclairs or ovals 1¼" by 2¾" (3 by 7 cm), or 1 large round Paris-Brest (see photos 15 and 16, page 83). Dust the pieces of dough lightly with the confectioners' sugar so that their shapes will be more even after baking.

Bake as soon as the dough is ready. Bake each sheet at 425°F (220°C) for the first 15 minutes, then lower the heat to 400°F (200°C) for the next 15 minutes. This change in temperature will prevent the puffs from cracking open, but be sure to keep the oven door ajar with a spoon. Watch the baking to see that the puffs are slightly moist. Small puffs bake faster than the larger ones, such as Paris-Brest or Saint-Honoré.

82

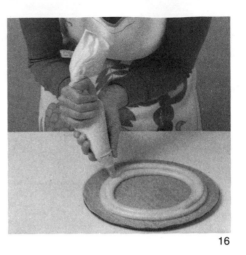

15 16

Note: Since the cooked puffs keep well, you should prepare and bake all the dough you make rather than trying to reserve leftover dough for later use.

To Store: The puffs can easily be kept a week in plastic bags in the refrigerator. They can be kept 1 month in the freezer but be sure to defrost frozen puffs for 24 hours in the refrigerator before using.

♕ ♕

47

Chiboust Pastry Cream

Chiboust cream is a light pastry cream mixed with an Italian meringue. Everything must be done rapidly, so have all your ingredients ready before beginning.

PREPARATION   30 minutes

For approximately 4 cups (300 g) cream
  For pastry cream
1 cup (¼ l) milk
½ vanilla bean
3 egg yolks
2½ tablespoons (35 g) granulated sugar
2 tablespoons (20 g) cornstarch
  For meringue
⅓ cup, scant (70 g), granulated sugar
2 tablespoons water
4 egg whites = ½ cup (120 g)
5 teaspoons (25 g) granulated sugar

Pastry bag with ¾″ (2 cm) round metal nozzle
Small saucepan
Candy thermometer [optional]
Electric mixer
2 large bowls

Making the Pastry Cream: Prepare the pastry cream base using the above-listed ingredients but following the instructions for vanilla pastry cream (Recipe 2). This pastry cream is less sweet than the classic recipe. Keep the cream hot; cover it to prevent a skin from forming on top.

Making the Meringue: Place the larger amount of sugar with the water in a small saucepan. Bring to a boil, stirring until the sugar is dissolved. As the sugar cooks, beat the whites until very stiff, adding the smaller amount of sugar halfway through. This should take about 5 minutes. Check the sugar. When it reaches 248°F (120°C) or the hard ball stage, it is ready to use. (If you don't have a candy thermometer, let a drop of sugar fall from a spoon into a glass of cold water; the sugar should form a ball and hold its shape on the bottom of the glass.) With the mixer on high speed, pour the boiling sugar into the egg whites, being careful not to let it fall on the edge of the bowl or on the beaters.

Reduce the mixer to low speed and add the boiling pastry cream. Beat just long enough to blend the two mixtures together. Transfer the cream to a second bowl or directly into a pastry bag—this will cool it off and prevent it from becoming grainy.

Chiboust pastry cream should be used as soon as possible after being prepared. A Saint-Honoré, a Paris-Brest, or individual puffs may be decorated with it. It is important to fit the pastry bag with a large nozzle—star shaped or not—since using a smaller nozzle would place too much pressure on the cream and make it fall apart. Once decorated the dessert should be chilled for at least one hour before being served.

To Store: Chiboust pastry cream must be eaten within 24 hours of being made. Keep desserts decorated with it refrigerated until served.

48

Paris-Brest

(Photo page 86)

This cake can be filled with any of 3 different creams. Prepare several rings of dough; they can be frozen easily or they will keep fresh for at least 1 week, if kept refrigerated.

PREPARATION | 40 minutes

BAKING TIME | 30 minutes

INGREDIENTS

For 1 cake, 6 servings
⅔ cup (300 g) cream puff pastry (Recipe 46)
⅓ cup (50 g) chopped almonds *or*
½ cup, generous (50 g), slivered almonds

For the Paris-Brest cream filling
1 cup (250 g) vanilla pastry cream (Recipe 2)
3½ tablespoons (50 g) butter, softened
½ cup (75 g) caramelized almonds (powdered)
Confectioners' sugar

For the Chiboust pastry cream filling
3⅓ cups (250 g) Chiboust pastry cream (Recipe 47)
Confectioners' sugar

For the light pastry cream filling
¾ cup (200 g) vanilla pastry cream (Recipe 2)
¾ cup (100 g) Chantilly cream (Recipe 1)
Confectioners' sugar

UTENSILS

Serrated knife
Wooden spoon
Baking sheet
Waxed paper [optional]
Pastry bag with ½″ (1 cm) nozzle and pastry bag with ¾″ (2 cm) star-shaped nozzle
Sugar dredger

85

Preheat the oven to 450°F (230°C).

On a buttered baking sheet, or a sheet lined with waxed paper, draw an 8″ (20 cm) circle or 12 small circles 2½″ (6 cm). With a pastry bag fitted with the ½″ (1 cm) nozzle, draw a circle of cream puff pastry dough on the baking sheet (see photo 16, page 83). Draw a second circle inside and touching the first one, then place a third circle on top of the 2 other circles. Dust the rings with the chopped or slivered almonds.

Bake for about 30 minutes, keeping the oven door ajar with a wooden spoon. Begin by baking at 450°F (230°C) until the cake has risen (about 15 minutes), then lower the temperature to 400°F (200°C). When the cake has cooled, cut the cake in half so that you can fill it.

Assembling the Cake: Fill the cake with the cream of your choice. Sprinkle generously with confectioners' sugar and refrigerate. Serve the same day. The following are instructions for three possible fillings.

Paris-Brest cream: Prepare the vanilla pastry cream; add the softened butter and the powdered candied almonds while the cream is cooling. Whip the cream for one minute at slow speed so that it becomes fluffy. Place in the pastry bag fitted with a ¾″ (2 cm) nozzle and use it to fill the cake.

Chiboust pastry cream: Prepare the cream and fill a pastry bag fitted with a ¾″ (2 cm) nozzle. The nozzle does not have to be star-shaped but it has to have a large enough opening so as not to flatten the light Chiboust cream.

Light pastry cream: Prepare the vanilla pastry cream and let it cool. Whip the Chantilly cream and fold it very delicately into the cooled pastry cream. Use the ¾″ (2 cm) nozzle with the pastry bag.

♕ ♕

49

Individual Paris-Brest

(Photo page 86)

The cream puff circles can be prepared a day ahead; they will keep fresh if kept in a sealed plastic bag. Any one of three different fillings can be used when making this cake. Choose from among three different kinds of fillings.

PREPARATION	30 minutes
BAKING TIME	30 minutes
INGREDIENTS	*For 10 individual Paris-Brest* ½ cup (200 g) cream puff dough (Recipe 46) ½ cup (80 g) chopped almonds

For the pastry cream filling
6½ tablespoons butter
⅓ cup (50 g) powdered caramelized almonds
¾ cup (200 g) vanilla pastry cream (Recipe 2),   cold
Confectioners' sugar

For the Chantilly cream filling
2 cups, generous (300 g), Chantilly cream (Recipe 1),
flavored with 2 teaspoons strong coffee
Confectioners' sugar

For the Chiboust cream filling
4 cups (300 g) Chiboust cream (Recipe 47)
Confectioners' sugar

UTENSILS   Pastry bag with ⅝" (1.5 cm) nozzle, round or star-shaped
Parchment paper
Serrated knife
Baking sheet
Wire whisk
Sugar dredger

Baking: Preheat the oven to 425°F (220°C). On a buttered or parchment pa-per-lined baking sheet, squeeze out six 2¼" (6 cm) circles of cream puff pastry, using a pastry bag with a ⅝" (1.5 cm) nozzle. Sprinkle the circles of dough with the chopped almonds. Bake for 30 minutes in a 425°F (220°C) oven, keeping the oven door ajar with a spoon. If, after 15 minutes, the cream puffs are too brown, lower the temperature of the oven to 400°F (200°C) for the remainder of the baking time. Remove from the oven and allow the puffs to cool.

Filling the Puffs: Using a serated knife, cut each puff in half and fill with one of the following:
   With the pastry cream: With a wire whisk, beat the butter and powdered caramelized almonds until a light creamy mixture is formed. Add the cold pastry cream and beat for another minute. Using a pastry bag with a ⅝" (1.5 cm) round or star-shaped nozzle, fill the bottom half of the cream puff circles with this cream. Place the other half on top and dust with confectioners' sugar.
   With the Chantilly cream-flavored with coffee: Fill the cakes and sprinkle with sugar as described above.
   With the Chiboust cream: Fill the cakes and sprinkle with sugar as described above.
   Refrigerate until ready to serve. These cakes should be eaten the day they are made.

50

Almond Cream Puffs

These are made with cream puff pastry filled with pastry cream, sweetened with powdered candied almonds. The cream puffs can also be filled with pastry cream flavored with rum, Kirsch or Grand Marnier.

PREPARATION	30 minutes
BAKING TIME	30 minutes
INGREDIENTS	*For 10 cream puffs*
	⅔ cup (300 g) cream puff dough (Recipe 46)
	½ cup (80 g) chopped, *or* 1 cup, scant (80 g), slivered almonds
	¾ cup (200 g) vanilla pastry cream (Recipe 2), cooled
	⅓ cup (50 g) powdered caramelized almonds
	6½ tablespoons (100 g) soft butter
	Confectioners' sugar
UTENSILS	2 pastry bags, one with ⅝" nozzle (1.5 cm) and one with ½" (1 cm) nozzle
	Parchment paper
	Sugar dredger
	Serrated knife
	Baking sheet
	Wire whisk
	Bowl

Baking: Preheat the oven to 425°F (220°C). Prepare the cream puff pastry dough.

On a buttered baking sheet (or one covered with parchment paper), squeeze out 10 round puffs 1½" (4 cm) using the pastry bag with the ⅝" (1.5 cm) nozzle. Sprinkle the top of each cream puff with the chopped or slivered almonds

Bake at 425°F (220°C) for 30 minutes, keeping the oven door slightly ajar with a wooden spoon. Meanwhile, place the pastry cream in a bowl and while beating with a wire whisk, add the powdered caramelized almonds and butter until you have a light and homogenous mixture.

Filling the Cream Puffs: To fill the puffs, cut open one side using a serrated knife. Place the pastry cream mixture in the pastry bag with the ½" (1 cm) nozzle, and fill the puffs with the cream.

Dust the cream puffs with confectioners' sugar and refrigerate. Serve them the same day they are prepared.

51

Saint-Honoré Chiboust

This is a ring of cream puff pastry, placed on top of flaky pastry and filled with the Chiboust pastry cream.

PREPARATION	1 hour
BAKING TIME	25 minutes
INGREDIENTS	*For 1 cake*

6¾ ounces (190 g) flaky pastry dough
   (either Recipe 36 or 37)
⅔ cup (300 g) cream puff pastry (Recipe 46)

For the Chiboust cream
   Pastry cream
1⅓ cups, generous (350 dl), milk
1 vanilla bean
5 egg yolks
3 tablespoons (45 g) granulated sugar
3 tablespoons (30 g) cornstarch
   Meringue
⅓ cup, scant (70 g) granulated sugar
2 tablespoons water
4 egg whites = ½ cup (120 g)
5 teaspoons (25 g) granulated sugar

For the caramel
¾ cup, generous (200 g), granulated sugar
3 tablespoons water

UTENSILS

Small saucepan
Baking sheet
Parchment paper [optional]
Mixing bowl
Wire whisk
Rolling pin
Wooden spoon
Fork
3 pastry bags with ⅝″ (1.5 cm), ½″ (1 cm) and ⅛″ (0.3 cm)
   nozzles
1 pastry bag with ¾″ (2 cm) star-shaped nozzle

Baking: On a buttered baking sheet (or one lined with parchment paper), roll a circle of flaky pastry dough that is 9½" (24 cm) round. Lift the dough up and let it fall to the table several times as you roll it out, to allow for shrinkage. When the right size, prick the dough all over with a fork.

Preheat the oven to 450°F (240°C).

Prepare the cream puff pastry and place it in a pastry bag fitted with the ⅝" (1.5 cm) nozzle. Make a circle of cream puff pastry on top of the flaky pastry dough. Alongside, on the baking sheet, make 16 small puffs using the ½" (1 cm) nozzle. If there is any dough left, make a spiral in the middle of the circle (see photo, page 90).

Bake for 10 minutes, then lower the temperature to 400°F (200°C) and bake for 15 more minutes, keeping the oven door ajar with a wooden spoon. Watch the color but try to avoid opening the oven door completely because the dough will fall. The small puffs will cook first—remove them after about 15 minutes of baking. When the large cake is done, remove from the oven and allow to cool.

Making the Chiboust Cream: While the dough is baking, prepare the Chiboust cream, following the instructions given for Recipe 47 but using the ingredients listed above. But, before adding the meringue, set aside ¾ cup (200 g) of the pastry cream to fill the cream puffs. Add the meringue to the remaining pastry cream.

Assembling the Cake: To fill the small puffs with the pastry cream, make a small hole in the bottom of the puffs with a knife and fill them with a pastry bag fitted with the ⅛" (0.3 cm) nozzle.

Prepare a very light caramel by mixing the sugar and the water in a small saucepan and heating until it begins to darken.

With the pan away from the heat, dip the tops of the puffs in the caramel (to avoid burning yourself, hold the small puffs on the tip of a knife) and place the puffs, caramel side down, on a buttered baking sheet (or on waxed paper) to cool. As soon as the puffs are cool (it will only take a couple of minutes), place them at regular intervals on top of the larger circle of cream puff pastry, attaching them with some more caramel.

Fill the center of the cake with the Chiboust pastry cream, using the pastry bag fitted with the ¾" (2 cm) nozzle. The nozzle need not be star-shaped but it should be large enough so as not to crush the cream.

Refrigerate the cake until you are ready to serve it. This cake should be served the same day it is prepared.

Pies and Tarts

Pies and tarts can be made with many doughs, but the two standard French doughs are Short Pastry and Sweet Short Pastry. The following recipes use Lenôtre's own versions of these doughs to make classics like Lemon Meringue Pie as well as some unusual creations like the Banana Tart. *Ed.*

♛

52

Short Pastry

This pastry dough is used to make pie and tart shells. The dough should be prepared a day in advance if possible.

PREPARATION	5 to 10 minutes
RESTING TIME	1 hour, minimum
BAKING TIME	15-25 minutes
INGREDIENTS	*For approximately 2 pounds (950 g) dough (3 9" tarts)*
	3¾ cups (500 g) flour
	1½ tablespoons (20 g) granulated sugar
	2 teaspoons (15 g) salt
	1⅔ cups (375 g) butter
	2 eggs
	2 tablespoons milk
	For approximately 12 ounces (350 g) dough (1 10" tart)
	1⅓ cups, generous (185 g), flour
	1½ teaspoons (7 g) granulated sugar
	¾ teaspoon (5 g) salt
	½ cup, generous (140 g), butter
	¾ beaten egg
	2¼ teaspoons milk
	For approximately 9 ounces (250 g) dough (1 9" tart)
	1 cup (140 g) flour
	1 teaspoon (5 g) granulated sugar
	½ teaspoon (4 g) salt
	6½ tablespoons (100 g) butter
	½ beaten egg
	2 teaspoons milk

Large mixing bowl
Electric mixer [optional]
Rolling pin
Parchment paper
Lentils for mold
Pie plates, metal flan ring, or whatever else is needed for
intended purpose

Making the Dough: *Using an electric mixer:* In a bowl, mix the salt and the sugar, add the butter in small pieces, then add the eggs and the milk. Beat the ingredients for a few seconds and then add all the flour at once.

Beat the ingredients just long enough to blend them. If the dough is worked too long, it will become elastic and tough when cooked. Don't worry if small pieces of butter are still visible.

Kneading by hand: Have all the ingredients measured and ready for use. Place the flour on the table in a mound, then make a well in the center of it. Sprinkle the sugar and the salt on the edges of the flour and in the well place the butter and the eggs. Mix all the ingredients together until crumbly, working

17   18

very quickly with the tips of your fingers (see photo 17). Then, knead the dough gently *(fraiser)* by pushing it away from you against the table with the palm of your hand (see photo 18). Add the milk as you do so. Gather the dough into a ball and *fraiser* once more, working as quickly and gently as possible. Form the dough into a ball, wrap it in a floured cloth or place in a covered bowl and let it stand for at least 1 hour, or if possible overnight, in the refrigerator; the dough will be easier to work the next day.

Roll out the dough on a lightly floured table. Line the pie shells or flan circle with the dough (see photo 19, page 95); either cut the excess dough off flush with the mold by rolling the rolling pin over the mold, or leave a smaller border and crimp it by pressing the dough against the mold at regular intervals with the blunt edge of a knife (see photo 20, page 95). Leave in a cool place for 1 hour before baking.

Baking: If you bake the shell empty, prick the bottom of it with a fork, then line the shell with parchment paper and fill it with lentils. This will prevent the dough from rising or forming bubbles as it bakes.

Once the shells are baked, remove the paper and the lentils; the lentils can be used in this way again.

If you decide to fill the unbaked shell with fruit and then bake it, do not prick the bottom of the shell because the juices will soak through the dough and make it soggy.

Note: To prevent the dough from becoming too elastic while working it by hand, first mix half the amount of butter into the flour until crumbly, work in the remaining butter, then continue the recipe as given above.

To Store: The dough will keep 8 days in the refrigerator. The pie shells can be prepared 24 hours before baking and filling.

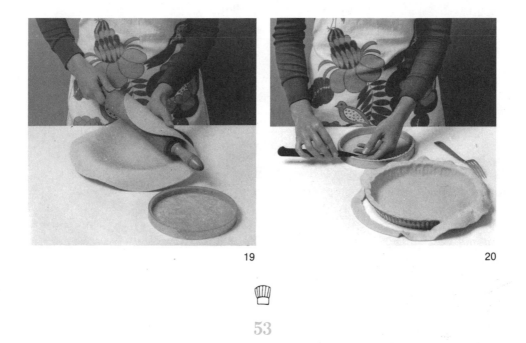

19   20

53

Sweet Short Pastry

This dough is very delicate and breaks easily; it is used for pie crusts or small tarts, as well as for cookies. It is best to prepare it the night before.

PREPARATION	15 minutes
RESTING TIME	1 hour
BAKING TIME	15-25 minutes

For approximately 2 pounds 10 ounces (1,200 g) dough
1½ cups (350 g) butter
½ cup (125 g) granulated sugar *or*
  ¾ cup (125 g) confectioners' sugar
1½ teaspoons (8 g) vanilla sugar
1 large pinch salt
3¾ cups (500 g) flour
1 cup (125 g) powdered almonds
2 eggs

For approximately 10½ ounces (300 g) dough
6 tablespoons (90 g) butter
2 tablespoons (30 g) granulated sugar *or*
  3 tablespoons (30 g) confectioners' sugar
¼ teaspoon, generous (2 g), vanilla sugar
1 pinch salt
1 cup, scant (125 g), flour
3 tablespoons (30 g) powdered almonds
½ beaten egg

Large mixing bowl
Electric mixer with dough hook
Plastic scraper
Rolling pin

Making the Dough: Place the butter between 2 sheets of plastic wrap or waxed paper, and tap it several times with a rolling pin to make it more workable.

Using an electric mixer: In a mixing bowl, blend together the butter (broken into pieces), sugar, vanilla sugar, salt, flour, and powdered almonds. Last of all, add the eggs.

Mix all the ingredients rapidly; this dough should not be worked for a long time. Wrap it well and let it stand for 24 hours in the refrigerator before rolling it out.

Kneading by hand: If kneading by hand, use the plastic scraper to cut and mix the dough. Follow the directions given for short pastry, Recipe 52.

Baking: Follow the directions given for short pastry, Recipe 52.

To Store: The dough will keep 15 days in the refrigerator if wrapped in foil.

To Freeze: You can freeze the dough for up to 2 months, if it is wrapped in foil. Before baking, defrost in the refrigerator for 24 hours.

54

Fruit Flan

(Photo page 98)

This flan is usually made in early summer with ripe red cherries but it can also be prepared all year round with fresh or stewed peaches, pears or cherries.

PREPARATION	10 minutes
RESTING TIME	1 hour
BAKING TIME	25 to 30 minutes
INGREDIENTS	*For 2 flans, 6 servings*
	10½ ounces (300 g) short pastry dough (Recipe 52)
	1 cup (¼ l) milk
	1 vanilla bean, split lengthwise
	6½ tablespoons (100 g) crème fraîche *or* heavy cream
	4 eggs
	¾ cup, generous (200 g), granulated sugar
	4 drops orange-flower water
	1 pound (450 g) fresh fruit *or*
	2½ cups (450 g) stewed fruit (if using stewed fruit, use only ½ cup, scant [100 g], sugar)
UTENSILS	Saucepan
	2 disposable aluminum pie pans, 8″ (20 cm) or 2 fireproof porcelain dishes
	Mixing bowl
	Parchment paper and lentils for the mold

Making the Filling: Roll out the dough and use it to line two lightly buttered pie pans. Refrigerate for at least 1 hour before baking (this can be done a day ahead).

Preheat the oven to 400°F (200°C).

Boil the milk with the vanilla bean for about one minute, then add the cream. In the mixing bowl, beat the eggs and the sugar together, then add the milk-cream mixture a little at a time, beating constantly. Stir in the orange-flower water. Place the bowl in cold water to cool the mixture while you beat it. Beat until the mixture is smooth and cold.

Baking: Bake the two pie shells without the filling by lining them with parchment paper, then filling the paper with lentils. Place in a 400°F (200°C) oven for 5 to 10 minutes, then carefully lift out the paper and the lentils.

Fill the half-cooked pie shells with the fruit, dicing the fruit if too large. Pour the creamy filling prepared earlier over the fruit. The pie pan should be no more than ¾ full. Bake in a 400°F (200°C) oven for 20 minutes. Serve warm or cold.

To Freeze: The flans can be frozen before baking. They can be baked without defrosting them but then add 5 to 10 minutes to the baking time.

55

Lemon Meringue Pie

(Photo page 100)

This tart's exquisite lemon filling is decorated with Italian meringue which is browned quickly under the broiler.

PREPARATION	40 minutes
BAKING TIME	25 minutes
INGREDIENTS	*For 8 servings* 10½ ounces (300 g) sweet short pastry dough (Recipe 53) *For the pastry cream* 1 cup (¼ l) milk ¼ vanilla bean, split lengthwise 3 egg yolks 2 tablespoons (30 g) granulated sugar 3 tablespoons (30 g) cornstarch Juice of 3 lemons Rind of 1½ lemons, finely grated *For the Italian meringue* 3 egg whites ¾ cup, generous (180 g), granulated sugar Confectioners' sugar, to glaze
UTENSILS	Mixing bowl Electric mixer Rolling pin Small saucepan Pie pan 8″ (20 cm) Lentils Parchment paper to line the dough Wooden spatula Pastry bag with ⅝″ (1.5 cm) star-shaped nozzle Sugar dredger Candy thermometer [optional]

Baking: Prepare the dough a day ahead. The next day, roll it out and line the pie pan with the dough. Cover the dough with the parchment paper and fill the paper with lentils. Bake for 25 minutes in a 425°F (220°C) oven. Remove and allow to cool. Remove the lentils and the paper.

Making the Filling: Prepare the pastry cream following the instructions given in Recipe 2 but using the ingredients given above. Once the cream is cooked and before it has cooled, stir in the lemon juice and grated rind.

To prepare the meringue, beat the egg whites until very firm, adding halfway through 1 tablespoon granulated sugar. Meanwhile, place the remaining sugar and 3 tablespoons of water in a saucepan; bring to a boil; boil the mixture until it reaches the hard ball stage (248°F = 120°C) on a candy thermometer (to test, dip a spoon in the sugar and drop a little bit of sugar in a glass of cold water; if the drop forms a ball on the bottom of the glass, the sugar is ready). Cooking the sugar will take about 5 minutes. Begin beating the egg whites again and pour the cooked sugar into them. Add the sugar quickly and try to pour it between the side of the bowl and the beaters. Continue beating at a low speed until the mixture has cooled (about 5 minutes). Take ⅓ of the meringue and carefully fold it into the lemon pastry cream with a wooden spatula. Spread this mixture onto the pie crust. Place the remaining meringue in a pastry bag fitted with a star-shaped nozzle and squeeze it out into little peaks that cover the whole tart. Sprinkle with confectioners' sugar and place under the broiler for 2 minutes or until golden brown.

Note: To simplify preparing this tart, French meringue (Recipe 79) can be used instead of Italian meringue. Boil the milk with a little lemon peel and add more lemon juice to the pastry cream if you want a stronger-flavored filling.

100

56

Mirabelle Plum Tart

The mirabelles are small, yellow plums common in France. Any other sweet, firm plum could be used in making this recipe.

PREPARATION	20 minutes
BAKING TIME	35 minutes

INGREDIENTS

For 8 servings
1 pound (450 g) short pastry dough (Recipe 52)
1 pound 5 ounces (600 g) fresh mirabelles *or*
    3⅓ cups (600 g) canned mirabelles
3½ tablespoons (50 g) butter
¼ cup (60 g) granulated sugar
2 tablespoons mirabelle-flavored brandy (*or* plum brandy)
2 cups (350 g) almond pastry cream (Recipe 5)
1 egg, beaten

UTENSILS

Pie pan 10½″ (26 cm) wide
Knife
Pastry brush
Rolling pin
Frying pan

Assembling the Tart: Set aside a little more than ¹/₅ of the dough, then roll out the remaining dough and use it to line the pie pan. Refrigerate the dough in the pie pan while preparing the fruit.

Pit the fresh mirabelles or drain them if they are canned. In a frying pan, melt the butter and the sugar; add the fruit and cook for 5 minutes, then add the mirabelle brandy and ignite. Remove from the heat and allow to cool.

Preheat the oven to 425°F (220°C).

Place the almond cream on top of the pie crust, then lay the mirabelles on top of it, placing them very close together. Roll out the dough put aside in the beginning and cut it into long strips.

Decorate the top of the tart with the strips of dough, forming a criss-cross pattern and sticking the ends of each strip to the edges of the tart by wetting them slightly. Brush the top of the tart with beaten egg.

Bake at 425°F (220°C) for about 35 minutes, or until golden brown. Turn out while still warm and serve immediately.

Note: If canned fruit is used, use only 2 tablespoons of sugar.

Banana Tart

PREPARATION	20 minutes
BAKING TIME	20 to 25 minutes
INGREDIENTS	*For 8 servings*

INGREDIENTS

For 8 servings
10½ ounces (300 g) sweet short pastry dough (Recipe 53)
⅔ cup (150 g) granulated sugar
⅔ cup (1½ dl) water
6½ tablespoons (1 dl) rum
5 ripe bananas
1½ cups, generous (400 g), vanilla pastry cream (**Recipe** (Recipe 2)

For the sauce
2¾ cups (500 g) canned pineapple (drained) *or*
   1 fresh pineapple, weighing 1¾ pounds (800 g), cored
   and sliced, plus ½ cup, scant (100 g), granulated sugar

UTENSILS

Pie pan 10½″ (26 cm)
Rolling pin
Large frying pan
Parchment paper, lentils to line the dough

Assembling the Tart: Prepare the dough a day ahead. Roll it out and line the pie pan the day you make the tart. Refrigerate it for an hour in the pie pan.

Preheat the oven to 425°F (220°C). In a large frying pan, mix the sugar, water and rum. Bring to a boil.

Peel the bananas and cut them in ½″ (1 cm) thick slices. Place the banana slices into the frying pan with the liquid and simmer very slowly for 10 minutes.

Meanwhile, prick the dough with a fork, line it with parchment paper, and fill the paper with lentils. Bake for 25 minutes in a 425°F (220°C) oven. Remove the paper and lentils when the dough is cooked. During the baking, prepare the pastry cream and let it cool. Fill the cooked pie crust with the pastry cream, then cover the cream with the drained banana slices, placed neatly close together.

Prepare a pineapple sauce in a blender, using either canned pineapple or fresh pineapple and sugar. Blend until the sauce is smooth. Cover the whole cake with a little of this sauce and serve the remaining sauce in a sauce boat. Serve immediately.

Note: The tart can be glazed with apricot jam instead of being coated with the pineapple sauce and other fruits (i.e., peaches, strawberries, etc.) can be used instead of pineapple to make the sauce.

Pear or Peach Tart with Almonds

PREPARATION	15 minutes
BAKING TIME	30 minutes
INGREDIENTS	*For 8 servings* 12 ounces (350 g) short pastry dough (Recipe 52) 2 cups (350 g) almond cream (Recipe 5) 4 large canned pears *or* canned peaches Apricot jam, to glaze
UTENSILS	Flan ring or pie pan 10½″ (26 cm) Rolling pin Pastry brush Knife

Baking: Preheat the oven to 425°F (220°C).

Roll out the dough and line the mold; fill with the cold almond cream. Cut each half-fruit in thin slices, crosswise, then make a star with the fruit on top of the cream (see photo, page 105). Bake 30 minutes at 425°F (220°C). Remove from the pan while still warm. When the tart is cold, brush on the jam.

59

Fruit Tartlets - Basic Recipe

PREPARATION	10 minutes
BAKING TIME	20 minutes
INGREDIENTS	*For 10 tartlets* 10½ ounces (300 g) of sweet short pastry dough (Recipe 53) 2 cups, generous (400 g), almond cream (Recipe 5) 1⅓ to 2 cups (250-400 g) fresh *or* stewed fruit ⅓ cup (100 g) apricot jam, warm
UTENSILS	10 metal circles 3″ (8 cm) or 10 small rectangular tartlet pans Baking sheet Pastry brush Rolling pin

Preparing the Tartlets: Roll the cold dough out on a lightly floured table. Line the pans or the circles and place them on a baking sheet; refrigerate for 1 hour.

Preheat the oven to 425°F (220°C).

Fill each tartlet with almond cream, then add the fruit (or fill the tartlets with fruit, then add the cream—see recipes that follow) and bake for 15 minutes.

Turn out while still warm. Glaze the tarts right away with the warm apricot jam.

60

Cherry Tartlets

PREPARATION	10 minutes

BAKING TIME   20 minutes

INGREDIENTS   *For 10 tartlets*
½ pound (250 g) cherries
Ingredients and utensils used in Recipe 59

Preparing the Tartlets: Follow basic Recipe 59. Before baking, cover the almond cream with the fresh pitted cherries. Finish as described earlier.

61

Peart Tartlets

(Photo page 107)

PREPARATION   10 minutes

BAKING TIME   20 minutes

INGREDIENTS   *For 10 pear tartlets*
½ pound (250 g) pears
Ingredients and utensils used in Recipe 59

Preparing the Tartlets: Follow Recipe 59 . Before baking the tarts, fill them with almond cream and garnish them with thin slices of pears.

Note: The tartlets can be garnished after they are cooked if you are using stewed fruit.

62

Sunshine Tartlets

(Photo page 107)

These are tartlets filled with pastry cream and pears.

PREPARATION	25 minutes
BAKING TIME	15 minutes
INGREDIENTS	*For 10 tartlets* 10½ ounces (350 g) sweet short pastry dough (Recipe 53) 2 cups (500 g) vanilla pastry cream (Recipe 2) 7 ounces (200 g) fresh or stewed pears Granulated sugar, for glazing
UTENSILS	10 tartlet pans or metal flan circles 3″ (8 cm) wide Rolling pin Parchment paper Lentils Flexible blade-spatula Baking sheet

Baking: On a lightly floured board, roll out the dough very thin. Line the pans or the circles with the dough and place them on a baking sheet. Prick the bottom of the dough and let it stand for 1 hour.

Preheat the oven to 400°F (200°C). Line the tartlets with parchment paper and fill them with lentils. Bake the tartlets 15 minutes, then remove from the oven and allow to cool. Remove the lentils and the paper. Turn out the pastry.

Filling and Decorating: Peel the pears and slice very thin. Spread a little pastry cream on the bottom of each pastry shell and put the sliced pears on top. Spread another layer of pastry cream on top of the pears, smoothing it over the top in a dome-like mound. Sprinkle generously with granulated sugar and caramelize the sugar by placing the tartlets under the broiler for a minute. The tartlets should only be assembled and caramelized at the last minute. Serve immediately.

Note: This recipe can also be prepared with fresh or stewed peaches, pineapple, bananas, strawberries, cherries, raspberries, or with stewed gooseberries or apricots.

♛

63

Mirabelle Plum Tartlets

(Photo page 74)

PREPARATION   10 minutes

BAKING TIME   20 minutes

INGREDIENTS   *For 10 mirabelle tartlets*
10½ ounces (300 g) mirabelles, *or* small plums of your choice (fresh *or* stewed)
Ingredients and utensils used in Recipe 59

Preparing the Tartlets: Follow the basic Recipe 59. Cover the almond cream with the drained fruit before baking. Finish as described earlier.

♛

64

Blueberry Tartlets

(Photo page 74)

PREPARATION   10 minutes

BAKING TIME   20 minutes

INGREDIENTS   *For 10 blueberry tartlets*
14 ounces (400 g) stewed blueberries
Ingredients and utensils used in the Recipe 59

Preparing the Tartlets: Follow the basic Recipe 59. Bake the tarts with the almond cream and cool. Garnish with the drained cooked blueberries.

Apricot Tartlets
(Photo page 107)

PREPARATION	10 minutes
BAKING TIME	25 minutes
INGREDIENTS	*For 10 apricot tartlets*

10½ ounces (300 g) short pastry dough (Recipe 52) *or*
   10½ ounces (300 g) sweet short pastry dough (Recipe 53)
⅔ cup (100 g) cookie crumbs
30 to 40 fresh or canned apricot halves
¾ cup, generous (200 g), granulated sugar (only if you use
   fresh fruit)
⅓ cup (100 g) apricot jam

UTENSILS   Same as Recipe 59

Preparing the Tartlets: Preheat oven to 400°F (200°C).

Line the tartlet pans or circles with the short pastry or the sweet short pastry. Sprinkle cookie crumbs over the bottom of each tartlet (they will absorb the fruit juices during baking). Place the apricot halves into each tartlet (the apricots should overlap each other). If you use fresh fruit, sprinkle the fruit with granulated sugar. Bake for 25 minutes and turn out while still hot. Using a pastry brush, glaze the tarts with warm apricot jam.

Miniature Fruit Tartlets

(Photo page 74)

PREPARATION	20 minutes
BAKING TIME	8 to 10 minutes
INGREDIENTS	*For 20 tartlets*
	8½ ounces (240 g) short pastry dough (Recipe 52)
	1 cup (200 g) almond cream (Recipe 5)
	10 apricots *or* 40 cherries *or* 5 pears *or*
	20 wedges of pineapple
	⅓ cup (100 g) apricot jam, warm
UTENSILS	20 small tartlet pans or circles
	Pastry brush
	Cookie cutter (a little larger than the pans or circles)
	Fork
	Rolling pin

Assembling the Tart: On a lightly floured table, roll out the cold dough and cut it with a cookie cutter slightly larger than the circles or tartlet pans.

Line the molds with the dough and prick the bottom with a fork. Fill each tartlet with almond cream.

Filling and Baking: Preheat the oven to 400°F (200°C). Choose one of the following two procedures:

I. Place on top of the cream in each tartlet either half an apricot, 2 or 3 cherries, or a quarter of a pear, sliced very thin. Push the fruit slightly into the cream. Bake in a 400°F (200°C) oven for 8 to 10 minutes. Turn out and allow to cool, then brush each tartlet with apricot jam and refrigerate before serving.

II. Bake the dough filled with the almond cream (without the fruit) for 8 to 10 minutes in a 400°F (200°C) oven. Turn out and allow to cool, then place on top of the cream a wedge of pineapple. Brush each tartlet with a little apricot jam and refrigerate before serving.

Genoise Cakes and Pastries

This chapter treats three very similar batters fundamental to the art of pastry making in France: the Génoise, Lady Finger, and Jelly Roll batters, each used in very different ways. The French idea of a layer cake is to take one airy genoise and carefully cut it into two, three, or even four thin layers. A rich butter cream is generally used as a filling for these spectacular creations. The lady fingers form the base for delicious charlottes — either fruit-flavored or other — and the jelly roll dough, spread with butter cream, rolled up, iced with yet more butter cream and decorated with Swiss meringue figurines, becomes the famous Yule Log to be seen in every French pastry shop at Christmas time. *Ed.*

67

Génoise

The Génoise is used to make many cream-filled cakes and desserts, but it can also be eaten plain.

PREPARATION	20 minutes
BAKING TIME	30 minutes
INGREDIENTS	*For 2 8″ (20 cm) cakes*
	⅔ cup (155 g) granulated sugar
	5 whole (1 cup) eggs
	3 tablespoons (45 g) butter
	1¼ cup, scant (155 g), flour
	1½ teaspoons (8 g) vanilla sugar
	For 1 8″ (20 cm) cake
	⅓ cup (78 g) granulated sugar
	3 whole (½ cup) eggs
	1½ tablespoons (23 g) butter
	½ cup, generous (78 g), flour
	1 teaspoon, scant (4 g), vanilla sugar

Mixing bowl
Electric mixer
Wire whisk
Large pot
Small saucepan
Wooden spatula
Flour sifter
2 8″ (20 cm) round cake pans

The Batter: Preheat the oven to 350°F (180°C). Place the eggs and sugar in a mixing bowl and set the bowl over a pot of boiling water; the water should not touch the bowl. Beat the eggs and sugar together for 1 minute, with the wire whisk. Then, with the bowl away from the heat, beat with the mixer at high speed for 2 minutes, then for 5 minutes more at low speed or until the mixture is very pale and falls from the wooden spoon in a smooth ribbon.

Clarify the butter in a small saucepan. Sift the flour and vanilla sugar, then fold into the egg-sugar mixture. Fold in the warm butter. Stop mixing as soon as all of the ingredients are well blended. This step should be done quickly and the Génoise should be baked right away.

Baking: Pour the batter into the buttered and floured pans and bake for 30 minutes or until golden brown. Let the cake cool for about 10 minutes, then turn out onto a rack, while still warm. Let cool completely before using.

Note: Do not overheat the egg mixture in the double boiler or the Génoise will dry out too fast when baking. For instructions on cutting the Génoise into layers, see the entry for Layer Cakes in the Dictionary of Terms and Procedures.

To Store: The Génoise will keep fresh for 8 days in the refrigerator if wrapped well in plastic or foil.

To Freeze: The Génoise will keep for 1 month if wrapped well, but be sure to allow it to thaw completely for 24 hours in the refrigerator before using it.

68

Strawberry Cake

This cake is filled with a butter cream filling and fresh strawberries, then topped with a layer of almond paste.

PREPARATION   **25 minutes**

INGREDIENTS   *For 1 cake, serving 6 persons*
1½ cups (300 g) butter cream filling (Recipe 7)
1 Génoise cake, (Recipe 67) either 6″ (15 cm) square *or* 8″ (20 cm) round
⅔ cup (1 ½ dl) dessert syrup, flavored with Kirsch (Recipe 11)

10½ ounces (300 g) fresh, small strawberries (some cut in half) for the filling
6 large strawberries

For the decoration
⅓ cup (100 g) red currant jelly and
12 large strawberries *or*
    5¼ ounces (150 g) almond paste decoration (Recipe 19)

UTENSILS

Pastry brush
Flexible blade-spatula
Bowl
1 piece of cardboard 8″ (20 cm) round or 6″ (15 cm) square
Serrated knife
Pastry bag with star-shaped nozzle [optional]
Rolling pin

Assembling the Cake: If you prepared the butter cream filling a day ahead, take it out of the refrigerator one hour before using it. Cut the Génoise in half with a serrated knife. Place the bottom half on the cardboard and, using the pastry brush, soak the cake with the dessert syrup. Spread a layer of butter cream filling on the cake to a thickness of between ⅛″ and ¼″ (3 mm to 5 mm).

Place whole strawberries all over the cream and those cut in half along the edges of the cake. All the strawberries should be "standing" on their base in the cream (see photo, page 115). Cover the strawberries completely with a second layer of butter cream filling.

Place the second layer of Génoise on top of the butter cream filling and soak this layer of cake with the dessert syrup, using a pastry brush. Cover this layer completely with another thin layer of butter cream filling.

Decorating: Either dip the 12 large strawberries into red currant jelly and place them on top of the cake, then cover the entire cake with the red currant jelly, or decorate the cake with almond paste in one of the following ways.

Use green-colored almond paste, and roll it out until you have a sheet large enough to cover the top of the cake *or* (if the strawberries around the side of the cake aren't perfectly even and erect) roll out enough almond paste to wrap around the sides of the cake as well.

Once the almond paste has been applied, cover the top of the cake with roses made from the butter cream filling or any other decorations made with the pastry bag. You could also place a multi-colored almond braid (see photo, page 27) on top, then place some large strawberries alongside and coat them with red currant jelly. Refrigerate the cake before serving. This cake should be eaten the same day it is prepared, or the following day at latest.

116

69

Chocolate Marquise

This is a rich chocolate layer cake that is refrigerated before serving.

PREPARATION	25 minutes
RESTING TIME	1 hour

INGREDIENTS

For 1 cake, serving 8 persons
1 Génoise (Recipe 67)
1 cup (2½ dl) dessert syrup, flavored with vanilla
   (Recipe 11)
1 cup, generous (290 g), chocolate pastry cream
   (Recipe 4)
5 teaspoons (25 g) butter, creamed
¾ cup (225 g) chocolate icing (Recipe 15)

For the decoration
5 tablespoons Chantilly cream (Recipe 1) *or*
Confectioners' sugar

UTENSILS

Mixing bowl	Serrated knife
Wire whisk	Pastry bag with ¼″ (0.6 cm) nozzle
Flexible blade-spatula	or sugar dredger
Pastry brush	Cardboard disk 8″ (20 cm)

Assembling the Cake: With the serrated knife, cut the Génoise into 3 equal layers. Place the first layer on the cardboard disk or serving platter and brush with dessert syrup. Cover the cake with a layer of chocolate pastry cream, using the spatula to smooth the cream. Place a second layer of the cake on top of the first, brushing it with dessert syrup and covering it with chocolate pastry cream. Place the third layer on top, again brushing with dessert syrup.

Whip the remaining chocolate pastry cream with the creamed butter and, using the spatula, cover cake with cream. Refrigerate for 1 hour.

Decorating: Spread the chocolate icing on the whole cake. With the pastry bag, decorate the surface of the cake with Chantilly cream. Or decorate by dusting the chocolate icing with confectioners' sugar, using cut-outs such as stars or circles to form patterns on the top. Refrigerate until ready to serve.

To Store: This cake will keep for 48 hours in the refrigerator.

Confiture préparée selon
l'ancienne recette de ma
grand'mère Eleonore Lindt

This is a strawberry jam-filled cake, flavored with Kirsch and surrounded with meringue and almonds.

PREPARATION   20 minutes

BAKING TIME   A couple of seconds under the broiler

INGREDIENTS   *For 1 cake, serving 8 persons*
                    1 Génoise cake 8″ (20 cm) round (Recipe 67)
                    ⅔ cup (1½ dl) dessert syrup, flavored with Kirsch
                        (Recipe 11)
                    10½ ounces (300 g) French meringue (Recipe 79)
                    1 cup (350 g) strawberry jam
                    ⅓ cup (50 g) slivered almonds

UTENSILS   Cardboard disk 8¼″ (22 cm)
                    Flexible blade-spatula
                    Serrated knife
                    Pastry bag with ½″ (1 cm) nozzle

Assembling the Cake: With the serrated knife, cut the cake into 2 equal layers. Brush the cake with the cold dessert syrup.

Place a layer of Génoise on the cardboard disk, which should be slightly larger than the cake. With a pastry bag filled with French meringue, draw a circle around the rim of the cake. Fill the center with all the strawberry jam, spreading it with the spatula. The jam will be inside the meringue circle and will not run out. Cover the jam with a second layer of Génoise. Cover the entire cake with a ½″ (1 cm) layer of meringue. Sprinkle the surface of the cake with slivered almonds. Place the cake under the broiler for a few seconds to lightly color the meringue and brown the almonds. Serve the cake warm.

To Store: This cake will keep up to 24 hours in the refrigerator.

♨ ♨ ♨

71

Easter Cake

This is a Génoise filled with a very light cream cheese and decorated with cherries, strawberries or raspberries.

PREPARATION   **20 minutes**

RESTING TIME   **1 hour**

INGREDIENTS   *For 1 cake, serving 8 persons*
1 Génoise (Recipe 67)

For the dessert syrup
¾ cup, generous (200 g), granulated sugar
⅔ cup (1½ dl) water
2-3 drops vanilla extract *or*
   3 tablespoons (½ dl) Kirsch

For the filling
1¾ cups (250 g) Chantilly cream (Recipe 1)
3½ tablespoons (50 g) granulated sugar
⅓ cup (75 g) farmer's cheese
⅔ cup (200 g) raspberry jam

For the decoration
40 candied cherries or cherries in syrup *or*
   1¾ cups (200 g) fresh strawberries *or* raspberries
3 tablespoons (50 g) raspberry jelly *or* jam
Confectioners' sugar [optional]

UTENSILS   Flexible blade-spatula
Serrated knife
Pastry brush
Pastry bag with ½" (1 cm) nozzle
1 8" (20 cm) cardboard disk

Assembling the Cake: Using the serrated knife, cut the Génoise into 2 equal layers. Prepare the dessert syrup and allow it to cool. Mix the sugar and the farmer's cheese; then fold all but 3 generous tablespoons of the Chantilly cream

into the sugar-cheese mixture. Brush the 2 layers of cake with the dessert syrup. Place one layer on the cardboard disk or simply on a serving platter and cover with a layer of raspberry jam and a 1″ thick layer of cream-cheese mixture. Place the second cake layer on top of the filling and cover the whole cake with more of the cream-cheese mixture, smoothing the top and sides with the spatula. Fill a pastry bag with the remaining cream-cheese mixture and make a decorative border all around the top of the cake (see photo, page 121). Refrigerate for 3 hours.

With the remaining Chantilly cream, again smooth the sides of the cake and place the cake back in the refrigerator. The cake needs to be kept very cold.

Decorating: Place the cherries or the fresh fruit inside the border on top of the cake. Brush the fruit with jam or jelly or simply decorate the cake with fresh fruit and confectioners' sugar. Refrigerate before serving; serve the same day as prepared.

♜ ♜

72

Upside Down Orange Cake

PREPARATION	45 minutes
COOKING TIME	2 hours a day ahead, 20 minutes next day
RESTING TIME	2 hours
INGREDIENTS	*For 1 cake, 6 servings*
	4 oranges
	4 cups water
	2¾ cups (600 g) granulated sugar
	⅔ cup (1½ dl) dessert syrup, flavored with Grand Marnier (Recipe 11)
	Juice of ½ orange
	1 cup, generous (150 g), Chantilly cream (Recipe 1)
	1¼ cups (300 g) vanilla pastry cream (Recipe 2)
	1 Génoise (Recipe 67)
UTENSILS	Mixing bowl
	Electric mixer
	Saucepan
	Serrated knife
	Pastry brush
	8½″ (22 cm) cake pan

Preparing the Oranges: Cut the 4 oranges into very thin slices. Boil the water with the granulated sugar, then add the orange slices to the syrup and simmer slowly for 2 hours. Pour the oranges and the syrup into a bowl and leave until the next day.

Assembling the Cake: Prepare the dessert syrup (Recipe 11), flavored with the Grand Marnier and the juice of half an orange.

Whip the Chantilly cream. Set aside half of the orange slices for decorating the cake and cut the remaining ones into small pieces. Mix the pieces with the vanilla pastry cream, then fold the cream and oranges very delicately into the whipped Chantilly cream.

Butter the cake pan and dust with sugar. Line the mold with the orange slices, as shown in the picture on page 123. Half fill the mold with the orange-flavored pastry cream. Cut the Génoise into 2 layers with the serrated knife and brush both with the syrup. Place one layer on top of the pastry cream (trim it if necessary to fit the pan). Cover the layer with the remaining orange-flavored pastry cream and place another layer of Génoise on top. Press the cake with a dinner plate (with a small weight on top) and refrigerate for 2 hours.

To turn out, remove the plate and weight, dip the cake pan into hot water and turn it over onto a plate. Serve within 48 hours and keep refrigerated until ready to eat.

73
Ladyfingers

Ladyfingers are used to garnish Bavarian cream molds and charlottes; they are also delicious served with whipped cream, fruit purées, stewed fruit, and vanilla or chocolate creams.

PREPARATION   25 minutes

BAKING TIME   18 minutes per baking sheet, with 24 ladyfingers per sheet

For 24 ladyfingers
5 eggs
⅔ cup (150 g)
    granulated sugar
1 cup, scant (125 g),
    flour
Confectioners' sugar,
    to sprinkle on top

UTENSILS

2 mixing bowls
Electric mixer
1 spoon
Pastry bag with
¾″ (2 cm) round metal nozzle
Parchment paper
Baking sheet
Sugar dredger

21

The Batter: Preheat oven to 350°F (180°C). Separate the whites from the yolks. Place the yolks in a mixing bowl. With the electric mixer set at medium speed, gradually beat in all but 1½ tablespoons of the granulated sugar. Beat for three minutes or until the mixture is thick, pale, and forms a ribbon. Carefully stir in the flour with a spoon, working the mixture as little as possible.

In another bowl, beat the egg whites for one and a half minutes with the mixer set at a high speed. Add the remaining 1½ tablespoons of granulated sugar and continue beating one and a half minutes more, or until stiff.

Carefully fold the egg whites into the batter as quickly as possible.

Baking: Line 2 baking sheets with parchment paper. To make the paper stick to the baking sheets, place a little batter under each corner of the paper. Fill the pastry bag with the batter. Squeeze out 24 ladyfingers 3½″ long (9 cm) onto the baking sheet. Before baking, dust the ladyfingers with the confectioners' sugar. Bake for 18 minutes. After the first 12 minutes, check to see if the baking sheet needs to be turned in order to obtain even browning.

Note: If you do not have parchment paper, butter and flour the baking sheets before using them. You can add 4 teaspoons of vanilla sugar or 1 teaspoon of vanilla extract to the batter before folding in the egg whites. Two teaspoons of orange-flower water or the grated peel of ½ lemon could be added instead to the batter, especially if the ladyfingers are going to be eaten plain.

To Store: The ladyfingers will keep two to three weeks if placed in an airtight container.

To Freeze: You can also freeze the container with the ladyfingers. Before using them, however, let them thaw for 24 hours. Once thawed, the ladyfingers should be eaten within 3 or 4 days or else they will become moldy.

Chocolate-Vanilla Charlotte

This is a charlotte made with vanilla sauce, Chantilly, and chocolate mousse.

PREPARATION   **45 minutes**

RESTING TIME   **1 hour, 30 minutes**

INGREDIENTS   *For 4 to 6 servings*
1⅓ cups (3 dl) vanilla sauce (Recipe 12)
1½ teaspoons (2 sheets) gelatin, softened in 1½ table-
    spoons cold water
14 ladyfingers (Recipe 73)
2 cups (300 g) chocolate mousse (Recipe 6)
2¼ cups (325 g) Chantilly cream (Recipe 1)
Shaved or grated chocolate [optional]

UTENSILS   Ribbed brioche mold 8½″ (22 cm) wide or straight-sided
    charlotte mold 6¼″ (16 cm)
Mixing bowl
Electric beater
Vegetable peeler
Pastry bag with star-shaped nozzle

Assembling the Charlotte: Make the vanilla sauce as described in Recipe 12. Add the softened gelatin to the vanilla sauce while the sauce is still warm. Cool the sauce by placing the pot it cooked in into ice water. Stir the sauce frequently until the sauce is cold and quite thick. Meanwhile, lightly butter the sides of the mold and garnish with the ladyfingers, cutting them off at the rim of the mold. Fill the mold halfway with chocolate mousse. Refrigerate for 30 minutes.

Set aside ¾ cup (100 g) of Chantilly cream for later use. Fold the remaining Chantilly cream into the cold vanilla sauce. Pour this batter on top of the chocolate mousse and fill the mold completely. Refrigerate for at least 1 hour.

To turn out, dip the mold for a few seconds into hot water and turn it upside down on a platter. Decorate the top of the charlotte with the Chantilly cream reserved earlier. Using a pastry bag with a star-shaped nozzle, make a decoration with the Chantilly or, using a vegetable peeler, shave some chocolate and place it on top of the charlotte.

Note: When using ladyfingers to line a mold, it is easiest to bake them close together in a straight line—they will stick together after baking and be easier to handle while lining the mold. Individual ladyfingers may also be used.

♕ ♕

75

Peach or Pear Charlotte

PREPARATION   **20 minutes**

RESTING TIME   **2½ hours**

INGREDIENTS   *For 4 to 6 servings*
14 ladyfingers (Recipe 73)—see note, Recipe 74
1⅓ cups (3 dl) vanilla sauce (Recipe 12)
2 teaspoons (2½ sheets) gelatin, softened in 2 tablespoons cold water
2 cups (300 g) stewed peaches *or* pears, drained
2 cups, generous (300 g), Chantilly cream (Recipe 1)

UTENSILS   Ribbed brioche mold 8½" (22 cm) or straight-sided char-lotte mold 6¼" (16 cm)
Pastry bag with star-shaped nozzle
Paper circle to set in bottom of mold
Wire whisk
Mixing bowl
Pastry brush
Saucepan
Knife

Assembling the Charlotte: Lightly butter the sides of the mold with a pastry brush. Line the bottom of the mold with the paper circle. Line the sides with the ladyfingers, placed close together, then cut them off at the rim of the mold.

Warm the vanilla sauce, and add the softened gelatin to it. Place the pot containing the sauce into a bowl of ice water. Stir frequently until the sauce is cold and quite thick. Leave ⅓ of the fruit whole for decorating and reserve; cut the rest into quarters. Save ¾ cup (100 g) of the Chantilly for decorating as well, then mix the remaining Chantilly with the cold vanilla sauce.

Fill the mold with alternate layers of charlotte batter and quartered fruit, ending with the batter. Refrigerate for 2½ hours.

To turn out, dip the mold in hot water and turn it over onto a serving platter. Remove the paper. Using the pastry bag with a star-shaped nozzle, decorate the charlotte with the remaining Chantilly and the remaining whole fruit.

Note: This charlotte can be served with cold vanilla sauce or a peach or pear sauce (Recipe 14).

128

Jelly Roll Dough

This dough can either be simply filled with jam to make a jelly roll or decorated to form one large, or several small Yule logs.

PREPARATION	15 minutes
BAKING TIME	About 7 minutes
INGREDIENTS	*For 1 roll, serving 8 persons* 4 egg yolks ⅓ cup (75 g) granulated sugar ½ cup (75 g) flour 3 egg whites 1½ tablespoons (25 g) butter, melted
UTENSILS	Electric mixer Narrow wooden spatula or spoon 2 mixing bowls Parchment paper 1 jelly roll pan or baking sheet

The Batter: Preheat the oven to 450°F (240°C). In a bowl, place the yolks and the sugar. Beat for 3 minutes with the mixer set at medium speed, then stir in the flour. Beat the egg whites until stiff, adding 1 teaspoon of sugar halfway through. Pour the melted butter into the bowl with the egg yolks, then fold the egg whites into this mixture.

Baking: Spread the batter into a rectangle at least 10″x12″ (25x30 cm) and no more than ½″ (1 cm) thick over a thickly buttered paper placed on the baking sheet. The batter should be spread evenly in order to keep the dough from drying out in any one spot. Bake for 7 minutes.

When the cake is done, remove the paper from the baking sheet and turn it upside down onto a flat surface. Wet the paper with a brush dipped in water; 2 minutes later, remove the paper. Cover the cake with a cloth to prevent it from drying out and let it cool. The cake is now ready to be filled and rolled.

77

Strawberry Yule Log

This is a rolled cake decorated with Italian meringue.

PREPARATION   15 minutes

BAKING TIME   10 minutes

INGREDIENTS   *For 1 roll serving 10 persons*
1 jelly roll (Recipe 76)
⅔ cup (1½ dl) dessert syrup, flavored with Kirsch
     (Recipe 11)
1½ cups (500 g) strawberry jam
Confectioners' sugar
Almond paste decorations (Recipe 19)
Swiss meringue mushrooms (Recipe 20)

For the meringue
4 egg whites
1 cup, generous (250 g), granulated sugar

UTENSILS   **Large mixing bowl**
Electric mixer
Small saucepan
Candy thermometer [optional]
Glass
Flexible blade-spatula
Pastry brush
Fork
Sugar dredger
Baking sheet

Preparing the Meringue: Prepare the Italian meringue by beating the egg whites until very stiff; halfway through, add 2 teaspoons of the granulated sugar.

Boil the remaining sugar with 4 tablespoons of water until the syrup reaches 248°F (120°C)—hard ball stage. Use the thermometer to determine temperature or test by dropping one drop of sugar into a glass of cold water; if ready, it will form a ball and hold its shape at the bottom of the glass. Very quickly, pour the sugar onto the egg whites, being careful not to let the sugar fall on the edges of the bowl or the beaters. Keep beating at low speed for about 5 minutes or until the mixture has cooled.

Baking: Preheat the oven to 475°F (240°C).

Brush the cake with the dessert syrup and then spread the strawberry jam over it. Roll the cake up, then with a spatula, completely coat the cake with an even layer of Italian meringue. Sprinkle with confectioners' sugar. To decorate, draw lines on the meringue with a wet fork. The log is now ready.

Bake for about 10 minutes to harden the meringue and give it a golden color. Turn off the oven after 5 minutes if you see that the meringue is golden brown, but leave the cake in the oven for another 5 minutes to complete cooking.

Let the cake cool, then decorate with almond paste decorations and Swiss meringue mushrooms.

To Store: The Yule Log will keep for 4 days if refrigerated.

♛ ♛ ♛

78
Coffee-Flavored Yule Log

This is a rolled cake with a coffee mousse filling and almond paste decorations. Its elaborate decoration always delights children, especially at Christmas time when Yule Logs are traditionally made in France.

PREPARATION   15 minutes

RESTING TIME   1 hour

INGREDIENTS   *For 1 roll serving 10 persons*
                     2 cups, generous (500 g), butter
                     1½ teaspoons coffee extract
                     French meringue made with 3 egg whites, unbaked
                         (Recipe 79)
                     1 jelly roll (Recipe 76)
                     ⅔ cup (1½ dl) coffee syrup (Recipe 11).
                     3½ ounces (100 g) almond paste decoration, green
                         (Recipe 19)
                     10 Swiss meringue mushrooms (Recipe 20)

UTENSILS   Mixing bowl
                     Electric mixer
                     Flexible blade-spatula
                     Pastry bag with star-shaped nozzle
                     Sieve

Preparing the Mousse: Take the butter out of the refrigerator 1 hour before using it. Place the butter in a mixing bowl and whip it for a minute or two at low speed until it is very soft and light. Then add the coffee extract and carefully fold in the French meringue.

Assembling and Decorating the Cake: Brush the coffee syrup onto the cold jelly roll, then spread ¾ of the mousse over the surface of the cake. Roll the cake very tightly and refrigerate for 1 hour.

To decorate, cut two slices from the cake each about ¾" (2 cm) thick. Place these slices on top of the log to simulate two cut off branches of a tree. With a pastry bag fitted with the star-shaped nozzle, cover the cake with the remaining mousse. Decorate by placing Swiss meringue mushrooms on top. Cut holly leaves out of green-colored almond paste to decorate as well. Press some of the almond paste through a large sieve onto the log to simulate moss. You can also place small almond paste figurines on the log. Cover the two ends and the branches with sheets of almond paste. Refrigerate until ready to serve.

To Store: The Yule Log will keep 3 or 4 days in the refrigerator.

Meringue Cakes

Cakes are not always made with egg yolks, butter, and flour. In the following recipes, meringues are used to replace doughs for individual desserts as well as to make "layer cakes" of unrivaled lightness, often in combination with rich creams or chocolate mousse. *Ed.*

79

French Meringue

This basic meringue is used to make layers for meringue cakes as well as individual pastries.

PREPARATION   15 minutes

BAKING TIME   1 hour, 15 minutes

INGREDIENTS   *For 3 7" (18 cm) circles or 20 individual shells or 1 pound (450 g) meringue*
5 egg whites
1 tablespoon, generous (20 g), granulated sugar
½ cup (125 g) granulated sugar, mixed with 1 cup, scant (125 g), confectioners' sugar

For 12 individual shells or 10½ ounce (300 g) meringue
3 egg whites
2 teaspoons (12 g) granulated sugar
⅓ cup (75 g) granulated sugar mixed with ½ cup (75 g) confectioners' sugar

Mixing bowl
Electric mixer
Pastry bag with ¾" (2 cm) nozzle
Parchment paper
1 or 2 baking sheets

The Batter: Preheat the oven to 275°F (135°C). Beat the egg whites until very stiff; halfway through, add the smaller amount of granulated sugar. Sift the mixture of granulated sugar and confectioners' sugar together and fold into the egg whites.

Baking: Do not let the meringue sit; it tends to fall apart. Fill the pastry bag right away with it and squeeze it onto a buttered and floured baking sheet or onto a baking sheet lined with parchment paper (stick each corner of the paper to the pan with a dab of meringue). You can make 3 7" (18 cm) circles for the Autumn Meringue Cake or 20 oval shells 1¹/₂" by 2³/₄" (3.5 cm by 7 cm) (see photo 22) or 20 2" (5 cm) round shells to make small meringue cakes.

You can bake two sheets at once. Bake for 1 hour, 15 minutes. The meringues should be very light brown and completely dry on both the top and bottom, when done. If they brown too quickly, turn the oven down.

Note: When you use leftover egg whites, remember that 5 egg whites = ¾ cup (155 g) and 3 egg whites = ½ cup (90 g).

To Store: Meringues can be kept for 3 weeks in a metal box or a tightly closed container.

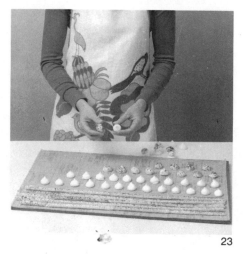

22

23

136

80

Concord Cake

This cake is made of chocolate mousse between three layers of chocolate meringue and covered with a chocolate meringue decoration.

PREPARATION	**40 minutes**
RESTING TIME	1 hour
BAKING TIME	1 hour, 5 minutes
INGREDIENTS	*For 1 cake, serving 10 persons for the meringues (including the decoration)* 3½ tablespoons (35 g) bitter cocoa powder 1 cup (150 g) confectioners' sugar 5 egg whites = ¾ cup (155 g) ⅔ cup (150 g) granulated sugar *For the mousse* 5½ ounces (160 g) semi-sweet chocolate 6½ tablespoons (100 g) butter 3 egg yolks 4 egg whites = ⅔ cup (120 g) 5 teaspoons (25 g) granulated sugar
UTENSILS	Pastry bag with ½″ (1 cm) nozzle Pastry bag with ⅛″ (0.3 cm) nozzle Mixing bowl and electric mixer Wooden spatula Baking sheet Sugar dispenser Parchment paper Flexible blade-spatula Oval cardboard 10″ by 5½″ (26 x 14 cm)

Preparing the Meringues: Preheat the oven to 300°F (150°C). Butter and lightly flour the baking sheet or cover the baking sheet with parchment paper. Mix the cocoa powder with the confectioners' sugar and sift together. Beat the egg whites until firm (about 5 minutes) adding 1½ tablespoons sugar halfway through. As soon as the egg whites are stiff, add the remaining sugar at low speed, then with the wooden spatula, quickly fold in the cocoa-sugar mixture.

Draw three ovals 10″ by 5½″ (26 x 14 cm) on the baking sheet to guide you when making the meringues. Take the pastry bag with the ½″ (1 cm) nozzle, fill it with chocolate meringue, and make three ovals by squeezing out the meringue in a spiral as shown in photo number 22, page 136. Once this is done, using another pastry bag with a ⅛″ (0.3 cm) nozzle, squeeze out all the remaining meringue into long strips as in photo 11.

Baking: Bake in a 300°F (150°C) oven for 1 hour and 5 minutes. Check the color of the meringue after 15 minutes of baking. The meringues should not brown. If they do, lower the heat of the oven. The meringue strips will be done first and should be removed while the large ovals might need 10 minutes extra baking. When they are cooked, the meringues are hard and can easily be detached from the baking sheet.

Both the ovals and the meringue strips can be prepared a day ahead.

While the meringue is baking, prepare the chocolate mousse following the instructions given with Recipe 6 but using the measurements listed above.

Assembling the Cake: Once the meringue has cooled completely, place one of the ovals on a decorative piece of cardboard, or simply place it on a serving platter.

With the flexible blade-spatula, spread a layer of chocolate mousse over the meringue. Then place on top of the chocolate mousse a second layer of meringue, then a second layer of chocolate mousse and finally the last layer of meringue. Cover the cake completely with the remaining mousse.

Cut the chocolate strips into ½″ (1 cm) sticks. Cover the sides and the top of the cake with these strips. Refrigerate for 1 hour. Lay a broad ribbon (or piece of cardboard) across the cake, then sprinkle the cake all over with powdered sugar. Remove the ribbon (this part of the cake will be darker since it was not covered with sugar) and serve.

To Store: The cake can keep 48 hours in the refrigerator.

♛ ♛ ♛

81

Autumn Meringue Cake

PREPARATION	30 minutes
COOKING TIME	15 minutes
RESTING TIME	1 hour minimum
INGREDIENTS	*For 1 cake, 6 servings* 3 circles of baked French meringue (Recipe 79) 2 cups, generous (300 g), chocolate mousse (Recipe 6) 5¼ ounces (150 g) semi-sweet chocolate
UTENSILS	Double boiler Flexible blade-spatula Flexible putty knife (see photo, page 140), 3½" (9 cm) wide at base Baking sheet Cardboard disk 7" (18 cm)

Assembling the Cake: Take half of the chocolate mousse and save for coating the outside of the cake. Place 1 layer of meringue on top of the cardboard disk and, using the spatula, spread a layer of mousse onto the meringue. Place the next meringue layer on top of the mousse and cover this second layer with another layer of mousse. Place the third meringue on top of the mousse. Cover the top and sides of cake with Chocolate mousse. Refrigerate 1 hour.

Decorating: Melt the chocolate in the double boiler, then with the putty knife, spread a *very* thin layer of chocolate onto the baking sheet. Chill.

After about 10 minutes, with the putty knife nearly horizontal to the baking sheet, scrape off a band of chocolate. The chocolate should form pleated ribbons 1½ to 2" (4 to 5 cm) wide; if the chocolate is too cold, it will break; in this case, let the chocolate stand at room temperature for 5 minutes and try again. If the chocolate is not cold enough, it will be too soft and you will not be able to pick it up; in this case, place the chocolate back in the refrigerator and let it harden some more before trying to form the ribbons. Once you have several bands of chocolate, place them around the sides of the cake, then begin to scrape chocolate to decorate the top. Try to get fan-shaped chocolate ribbons by placing your thumb against one edge of the chocolate ribbons as you scrape.

Form a circle with the least pleated strips of chocolate placed around the rim of the cake, and in the center, place the most fan-shaped strips to form a rose.

82

Succès Batter

PREPARATION 15 minutes

BAKING TIME 1 hour, 20 minutes

INGREDIENTS

For 2 8″ (20 cm) shells plus 2 6″ (15 cm) shells or 40 small shells
5 egg whites
1 tablespoon, generous (20 g), granulated sugar
¾ cup (170 g) granulated sugar
⅔ cup, scant (90 g), confectioners' sugar
⅔ cup (90 g) powdered almonds
3 tablespoons (5 cl) milk
Confectioners' sugar to sprinkle on top

For 2 8″ (20 cm) shells or 20 small shells
3 egg whites
2½ teaspoons (12 g) granulated sugar
½ cup, scant (100 g), granulated sugar
⅓ cup (55 g) confectioners' sugar
⅓ cup, generous (55 g), powdered almonds
2 tablespoons (3 cl) milk
Confectioners' sugar to sprinkle on top

UTENSILS

2 large mixing bowls
Electric mixer
Wooden spatula
Parchment paper
2 pastry bags: one with a ¾″ (2 cm) nozzle and one with
   a ½″ (1 cm) nozzle
2 or 3 baking sheets, depending upon your purposes
Sugar dredger

The Batter: Beat the egg whites until stiff; halfway through, add the smaller amount of granulated sugar. If you are using leftover egg whites and have forgotten how many you have, remember that 5 egg whites = ¾ cup (155 g) and 3 egg whites − ½ cup (95 g).

24   25

Preheat the oven to 275°F (135°C).

In a separate bowl, mix the larger amount of granulated sugar with the confectioners' sugar. Add the powdered almonds and the milk, then fold in a few spoonfuls of egg white. Pour this mixture on top of the remaining egg whites, and fold it in with a wooden spatula. Work carefully but quickly; there should be no particles of unblended egg white in the finished batter. Butter the baking sheets and dust them lightly with flour or line the sheets with parchment paper, sticking each corner down with a dab of batter.

Baking: *For large shells:* With a pencil, draw an 8″ (20 cm) circle and a 6″ (15 cm) circle on each baking sheet. Squeeze out the batter in a continuous spiral to fill the circles, using a pastry bag with a ¾″ (2 cm) nozzle (see photo 24). Dust the batter with confectioners' sugar and bake both baking sheets for 1 hour and 20 minutes. After 40 minutes, place the top baking sheet on the bottom and vice versa, so as to brown them both evenly.

For small shells: With a pencil, draw 20 1½″ (4 cm) circles on each pastry sheet to make small shells or Chocolatines. Fill each circle with the batter using a pastry bag with a ½ inch nozzle as described above. To prepare Succès, use the pastry bag set with a ¾″ (2 cm) nozzle and make mounds 1½″ (4 cm) in diameter. Dust them all with confectioners' sugar and bake both sheets at the same time for 45 to 50 minutes. Switch the sheets midway through the baking process.

Watch the browning of the Succès; you might have to lower the oven temperature because you find that they are browning too rapidly.

To Store: You can keep Succès for 15 days in a tightly sealed container.

144

♨ ♨ ♨

83

Almond Succès

*This beautiful white-topped cake can either be decorated with crushed cara-
melized almonds or simply wrapped in a gold-colored ribbon to give it a more
festive air before serving.*

PREPARATION	20 minutes
BAKING TIME	1 hour
INGREDIENTS	*For 1 cake, 6 servings* 4 cups (750 g) almond butter cream (Recipe 10) 2 baked Succès circles 8″ (20 cm) (Recipe 82) Confectioners' sugar ⅓ cup (50 g) crushed caramelized almonds [optional]
UTENSILS	8″ (20 cm) cardboard disk Flexible blade-spatula Sugar dredger Gold ribbon

Assembling the Cake: If the almond butter cream was prepared in advance,
then take it out of the refrigerator 1 hour before you intend to use it. Place one
of the Succès circles on the cardboard disk and cover it with 3¼ cups (600 g)
of the cream. Press, very lightly, when you cover the cream with the second
Succès circle. Cover the entire cake with the remaining butter cream, using
a spatula. Dust the top of the cake generously with confectioners' sugar. Refrigerate for 1 hour, then press the crushed caramelized almonds, if using,
around the sides of the cake or tie a large, decorative, golden ribbon around
the cake. Serve cold.

To Store: The cake will keep 3 to 4 days in the refrigerator.

84

Chocolatines

In this recipe, Succès pastry shells are filled with chocolate mousse and sprin-kled with chocolate flavored confectioners' sugar.

PREPARATION	30 minutes
BAKING TIME	1 hour
INGREDIENTS	*For 10 small cakes*
	20 baked Succès shells 2½″ (6 cm) (Recipe 82)
	2 cups (300 g) chocolate mousse (Recipe 6)
	⅓ cup (50 g) confectioners' sugar
	2 tablespoons (20 g) cocoa powder
UTENSILS	10 metal circles 2½″ (6 cm) wide and 1″ (3 cm) high
	Sponge

Assembling the Cake: In each metal ring, place a Succès shell. Cover with chocolate mousse, then put a second Succès shell on top and cover with choc-olate mousse. Refrigerate for 1 hour.

Remove from the refrigerator and rub a sponge dipped in hot water around each metal ring. Remove the rings. Mix the confectioners' sugar with the cocoa powder and sprinkle over the top of each cake. Serve the cakes the day they are prepared or, at the latest, the following day.

Note: A one-inch high band of cardboard can be used to form a ring and used instead of the metal ring. This cardboard ring is simply cut off after the cake has been refrigerated.

Crêpes, Soufflés, Creams, and Puddings

No one type of dough characterizes the desserts in this chapter. Here you'll find that the mystery of soufflés is solved, and learn how waffles can be turned into desserts both easy and delicious. Most of these recipes can be made at the last minute for quick, elegant desserts. *Ed.*

85

Crêpes Suzette

These crêpes are filled with an orange-flavored pastry cream and flamed with Grand Marnier.

PREPARATION	1 hour, 30 minutes
COOKING TIME	(with two crêpe pans): 20 minutes, plus 10 minutes when serving
INGREDIENTS	*For 30 crêpes, 6" (15 cm)* 5½ tablespoons (80 g) butter 1¾ cups (250 g) flour ⅓ cup (80 g) oil ¼ cup (60 g) granulated sugar 6 eggs 2 teaspoons Grand Marnier 1 orange peel, finely chopped 3 cups, generous (¾ l), milk 3⅔ cups (900 g) vanilla pastry cream (Recipe 2), flavored with 2 teaspoons Grand Marnier, juice of one orange, and 2 orange peels, finely chopped

For the syrup
⅔ cup (150 g) butter
⅔ cup (150 g) granulated sugar
Juice of 2 oranges
⅔ cup (1½ dl) Grand Marnier

2 platters, 16″ (40 cm) long
Aluminum foil
2 crêpe pans 6″ (15 cm) wide at the bottom
Saucepan
Wire whisk or electric mixer
Bowl
Spatula
Saucepan
Bowl and soup ladle
Very large frying pan, if possible

The Batter: Cook the butter until it is barely light brown and has a slightly nutty smell. In a mixing bowl, mix the flour, oil, sugar, eggs, Grand Marnier, rum, orange peel, melted butter, and 1 cup of milk. Beat until the mixture is smooth and continue adding all but 1 cup of the milk. Save this cup of milk for later. Flavor the pastry cream with the Grand Marnier, orange juice, and chopped orange peel.

Cooking and Serving: Make the crêpes in two crêpe pans, cooking them for about 1 minute on each side. Keep the crêpes warm once they are cooked. Prepare the syrup with the Grand Marnier; in a saucepan, melt the butter, add the sugar and the juice of 2 oranges and half the Grand Marnier (keep the other half warm in a small saucepan). Bring this mixture to a boil and remove from heat. Spoon a little of this syrup over the serving platter. Fill each crêpe with 1 generous tablespoon of pastry cream, roll, and keep warm on the serving platter, covered with aluminum foil. Just before serving, heat the remaining syrup in a large frying pan and place the rolled crêpes in the syrup. When the crêpes are hot, pour the remaining Grand Marnier into the skillet as well and light with a match. Serve the crêpes very quickly. (This last step should be done in front of guests because the crêpes will not flame for a very long time).

Note: It is advisable to mix either cognac or rum with the Grand Marnier used to flame the crêpes. This recipe can be simplified by not filling the crêpes with pastry cream. Simply fold the crêpes in four, place them in the skillet and pour the Grand Marnier syrup over them. Heat and pour a tablespoon of hot Grand Marnier over them, light and serve.

86

Waffles

PREPARATION   15 minutes

COOKING TIME   4 minutes per waffle

INGREDIENTS

For 20 small waffles
1½ cups (35 cl) milk
1 pinch salt
6½ tablespoons (100 g) butter
1¾ cups (250 g) flour
8 eggs
1 cup (¼ l) milk mixed with 1 cup (¼ l) heavy cream *or*
     1⅓ cups (3 dl) milk mixed with ¾ cup (2 dl) crème
     fraîche
Confectioners' sugar, jam, Chantilly cream (Recipe 1),
     or chocolate sauce (Recipe 13)

UTENSILS

Waffle iron
Saucepan
Mixing bowl
Electric mixer
Sugar dredger
Wooden spoon

The Batter: Heat the milk with the salt, add the butter and bring to a boil. Away from the heat, add the flour all at once and mix in with a wooden spoon. Put the batter back on the fire for a few seconds, stirring constantly until it comes away from the sides in a smooth mass and no longer sticks to the spoon. Pour into a mixing bowl and with an electric beater set at low speed, beat in the eggs two by two.

Still beating at low speed, add one of the milk-cream mixtures listed above.

Cooking: Heat the waffle iron and butter it lightly. With a ladle, fill the waffle iron and cook two minutes on each side, if using a hand held iron, or approximately four minutes total in an electric waffle iron.

Serve the waffles hot, sprinkled with confectioners' sugar or spread with jam, Chantilly cream, or chocolate sauce.

150

Chocolate Soufflé

This chocolate soufflé can be served with a chocolate sauce.

PREPARATION	20 minutes
BAKING TIME	20 minutes
INGREDIENTS	*For 3 to 4 servings*
	3 ounces (90 g) chocolate
	¼ cup (60 g) granulated sugar
	3 tablespoons milk
	2 egg yolks
	3 egg whites
	1½ tablespoons (20 g) granulated sugar
	Confectioners' sugar
	¾ cup (2 dl) chocolate sauce (Recipe 13)
UTENSILS	Soufflé dish 6″ (16 cm)
	Bowl
	Electric mixer
	Wooden spoon
	Sugar dispenser
	Knife
	Double-boiler
	Saucepan

Preparing the Soufflé: Preheat the oven to 350°F (180°C).

In a double-boiler, melt the chocolate, then add the sugar and the milk and beat until well mixed. Remove from the heat. Allow the mixture to cool for 5 minutes, then add the egg yolks, beating constantly. Whip the egg whites until very stiff, adding 1½ tablespoons (20 g) sugar halfway through. Fold the egg whites into the chocolate mixture.

Pour the mixture into a buttered and sugared soufflé mold. Bake 20 minutes at 350°F (180°C). Test for doneness by inserting a knife blade: if blade comes out dry, the soufflé is ready. Serve immediately, sprinkled with confectioners' sugar.

Note: If you serve the soufflé with a chocolate sauce, the sauce should be cool and served alongside in a sauce boat.

Caramel Almond Soufflé

(Photo page 152)

PREPARATION	20 minutes
BAKING TIME	20 minutes
INGREDIENTS	*For 3 to 4 servings*
	1 cup (¼ l) milk
	2½ tablespoons (40 g) granulated sugar
	¼ cup (40 g) flour
	1½ tablespoons (20 g) butter
	3 egg yolks
	⅔ cup (100 g) powdered caramelized almonds
	2 teaspoons rum
	4 egg whites
	1½ tablespoons (20 g) granulated sugar
	⅓ cup, generous (80 g), sugared almonds, coarsely crushed

Making the Soufflé: Preheat the oven to 350°F (180°C). Generously grease the mold, then coat the inside with granulated sugar. Measure out the milk, then set 3 tablespoons aside. Place the remainder in the saucepan and bring it to a boil.

In the mixing bowl, place the sugar, flour, and 3 tablespoons of milk and beat with the wire whisk. Add a little of the boiling milk and mix well, then pour the mixture into the saucepan with the boiling milk. Boil for 2 minutes, then remove from the heat.

Add the butter, cover the saucepan, and allow to cool for 15 minutes. Then, stir in the egg yolks with the wire whisk. Add the powdered caramelized almonds and rum.

Beat the egg whites until moderately firm, adding the granulated sugar half-way through. Gently fold the batter into the beaten egg whites with a wooden spatula.

Baking: Pour half the mixture into the buttered and sugared mold; sprinkle on the crushed sugared almonds, then pour in remaining soufflé mixture. Bake for about 20 minutes or until done.

To test for doneness, plunge the blade of a knife into the center of the soufflé. If the knife comes out clean, the soufflé is done.

Note: The batter can stand for as long as 30 minutes before being baked, if covered and kept warm (90° to 100°F or 30° to 40°C). You can bake more than one soufflé at a time; you can also prepare 4 individual soufflés, using the same recipe.

89

Apple Soufflé with Calvados

PREPARATION	20 minutes
BAKING TIME	25 minutes
INGREDIENTS	*For 4 servings or 4 individual soufflés* 1 cup (¼ l) milk ¼ vanilla bean ¼ cup (65 g) sugar ¼ cup (40 g) flour 1½ tablespoons (20 g) butter 1½ tablespoons Calvados (apple brandy) 3 egg yolks 2 apples 3 egg whites 1½ tablespoons (20 g) granulated sugar 1½ tablespoons Calvados for flaming
UTENSILS	Soufflé mold 7″ (18 cm) wide or 4 individual soufflé molds Electric mixer Mixing bowl Wooden spatula 2 saucepans

The Batter: Boil all but 3 tablespoons of the milk with the vanilla bean. In a mixing bowl, mix the sugar, the flour and 3 tablespoons of milk. Then add, stirring with a spatula, half the boiling milk, mix well; add the remaining boiling milk beating all the while. Pour back into the sauce pan and boil for 2 minutes more.

Away from the heat, stir in the butter and the Calvados, cover and allow to cool. When the batter has cooled, but is still warm, add the egg yolks.

Baking: Preheat the oven to 350°F (180°C).

Peel and cut the apples into very thin slices. Beat the egg whites until very stiff. Halfway through, add 1½ tablespoons (20 g) sugar, then fold the stiff egg whites into the batter prepared earlier. Butter and sugar the mold. Fill the mold with a third of the batter, then place a layer of apples on top of the batter. Add another third of the batter and a layer of apples. Finish filling the mold and place apple slices on top. Sprinkle the surface with confectioners' sugar. Bake the soufflé at 350°F (180°C) for 25 minutes.

Just before removing it from the oven, heat 1½ tablespoons of Calvados in a small saucepan and light. Pour the Calvados over the soufflé and serve immediately.

90

Snow Eggs

Elegant rose-shaped pieces of egg white are served on a vanilla sauce in this dessert.

PREPARATION	10 minutes
COOKING TIME	10 minutes per batch
INGREDIENTS	*For 6 servings* 6 egg whites ¾ cup, generous (200 g), granulated sugar 2⅔ cups (6 dl) vanilla sauce (Recipe 12)
UTENSILS	Pastry bag with star-shaped nozzle ¾″ (2 cm) Clean dish towel Large frying pan Large sheet of waxed paper Slotted spoon or spatula

Poaching the "Eggs": Simmer 2 quarts of water in a large frying pan. Do not let the water boil. Meanwhile, beat the egg whites until very stiff, then add the sugar and continue beating slowly for 30 seconds. Place a large sheet of waxed paper next to the frying pan. Dampen the paper lightly. Fill the pastry bag with the egg whites, and squeeze out large rose-shaped designs onto the paper (about 20 of them). Lift them one at a time very carefully with a spatula and slide them into the simmering water. Poach for 7 minutes on one side without allowing the water to boil; then, turn them over and poach again for 3 more minutes. Remove and drain on a dish towel. The "roses" should not touch one another while poaching. Poach in several batches and do not crowd the pan. When the "roses" are drained, place them on top of the cold vanilla sauce in a serving dish. Chill for at least 1 hour before serving. Don't place them on top of one another, since they might break.

91

Fruit-Flavored Bavarian Cream

This light vanilla-flavored dessert can be made in a ring mold or any other shaped mold of your choice.

PREPARATION	15 minutes
RESTING TIME	2 hours, minimum
INGREDIENTS	*For 4 to 6 servings* 2 cups (285 g) Chantilly cream (Recipe 1) *For the Bavarian cream* 1 tablespoon (4 sheets) unflavored gelatin 3 tablespoons cold water 2²/₃ cups (6 dl) vanilla sauce (Recipe 12), warmed *Optional* 1¹/₂ tablespoons Kirsch + 1 teaspoon (1 sheet) gelatin 1 cup (¼ l) raspberry sauce (Recipe 14) [optional] 1 pound 1½ ounces (500 g) mixed fresh fruit, to make a fruit salad
UTENSILS	1½-quart ring mold Pastry bag with star-shaped nozzle Bowl Wire whisk

Preparing the Cream: Set aside half of the Chantilly cream for decorating and refrigerate. Prepare the Bavarian cream by dissolving the gelatin in cold water, then adding the vanilla sauce; stir with a spatula and if desired, add Kirsch if adding Kirsch, use the extra gelatin in the beginning of recipe). Allow to cool.

When the Bavarian cream is completely cool (but not too cold) very delicately fold in the Chantilly. Slightly dampen the mold, then sprinkle the bottom and sides with granulated sugar (this will help when turning out the Bavarian cream). Cover the bottom of the mold with a thin layer of raspberry sauce [optional]. Then fill the mold up to the rim with the batter and refrigerate for at least 2 hours.

To turn out, dip the mold in hot water for a few seconds, then turn out onto a serving platter. Using a pastry bag with a star-shaped nozzle, decorate the Bavarian cream with the Chantilly cream reserved earlier. Serve the raspberry sauce in a sauce boat and fresh fruit salad at the same time.

Note: When using a ring mold, you can fill the center with fruit salad.

$\text鸮\text鸮$ (chef hat symbols)

🧑‍🍳 🧑‍🍳

92

Rice Pudding with Eight Treasures

The eight treasures are eight different candied fruits: dates, prunes, raisins, ginger, etc. (or others of your choice).

PREPARATION	1 hour
RESTING TIME	3 hours
COOKING TIME	35 minutes
INGREDIENTS	*For 8 to 10 servings* 1 cup (200 g) rice 3 cups, generous (¾ l), water 3 cups, generous (¾ l), milk 1 vanilla bean 3½ tablespoons (50 g) granulated sugar 1 piece candied ginger, 1½″ (4 cm) long 2⅔ cups (6 dl) vanilla sauce (Recipe 12)

2¼ teaspoons (3 sheets) gelatin, softened in 2 tablespoons
    cold water
1¾ cups (250 g) Chantilly cream (Recipe 1)
1½ cups (300 g) candied fruits (8 different kinds), diced
    very small
1 orange peel, diced
½ lemon peel, diced
1 cup (150 g) candied cherries
⅔ cup (100 g) stewed peaches
2 cups, generous (½ l), raspberry sauce (Recipe 14)

UTENSILS

1 ring mold 11″ (28 cm)
Pastry bag with star-shaped nozzle
Mixing bowl
Wire whisk
Spatula
Grater
Large saucepan

Cooking the Rice: Boil the rice for 2 minutes in the boiling water. Drain and rinse the rice under cold water to remove the starch. Meanwhile, in a heavy-bottomed saucepan, bring the milk to a boil with the vanilla bean split in two lengthwise. As soon as the milk boils, pour in the rice, the sugar and the ginger. Cover and cook for 25 minutes or until the rice has absorbed all the liquid. Remove the vanilla bean and the ginger and allow the rice to cool.

Assembling and Decorating: Set aside half the vanilla sauce in a sauce boat. Add the softened gelatin to the remaining warm vanilla sauce. Cool the vanilla sauce by placing the pot it cooked in into a bowl of ice water. Stir frequently, until the sauce is cold and quite thick. Set aside ¾ cup (100 g) of Chantilly cream and refrigerate. Add the remaining Chantilly cream to the cold vanilla sauce. When the boiled rice is cold, stir in the diced candied fruit, the orange peel, and the lemon peel. Fold this mixture very delicately into the Chantilly-vanilla sauce mixture. Slightly dampen the mold and sprinkle with sugar. Fill the bottom with candied cherries cut in half, then pour in the rice mixture. Refrigerate for 3 hours.

   To turn out, dip the mold for a few seconds in warm water and turn it over onto a serving platter. Decorate with sliced peaches. Using a pastry bag with a star-shaped nozzle, decorate the center with rose shape designs made with the Chantilly reserved earlier.

Caramel Custard

This caramel custard is served with vanilla sauce.

PREPARATION   15 minutes

BAKING TIME   40 minutes

INGREDIENTS   *For 8 servings of the caramel*
¾ cup, generous (200 g), granulated sugar
1½ tablespoons water
3 drops lemon juice

For the custard
4⅓ cups (1 l) milk
1 vanilla bean
4 eggs
8 egg yolks
¾ cup, generous (200 g), granulated sugar
1⅓ cups (3 dl) vanilla sauce (Recipe 12)

UTENSILS   Soufflé mold 8½″ (22 cm) wide or charlotte
                    mold 7″ (18 cm) wide
                    Mixing bowl
                    Wire whisk
                    Small saucepan

Assembling and Baking: Make the caramel in a small saucepan by heating the sugar, water, and lemon juice until the mixture is golden brown (about 8 to 10 minutes). Pour the caramel into the mold, turning the mold so that the caramel covers both the bottom and the sides.

Preheat the oven to 400°F (200°C).

Boil the milk with the vanilla bean. In a mixing bowl, beat the eggs, the egg yolks, and the sugar. Stirring constantly, stir the hot milk into the egg mixture. Pour this custard into the mold and bake in a bain-marie for 40 minutes at 400°F (200°C). To be sure the cream is cooked, insert a knife blade into the cream; if the blade comes out clean, the cream is done. Remove from the oven and cool. Turn out the caramel custard onto a platter and serve with a vanilla sauce on the side.

Note: Try the following variations: instead of pouring the caramel into the mold, pour it into the boiling milk, mixing it gently. In this case, butter the mold and sprinkle some sugar into it before adding the custard. Or you might want to butter the mold and sprinkle with sugar, then fill the mold with the custard. Prepare the caramel as described above and pour it over the top of the custard before baking.

Apple Charlotte

Use tart cooking apples and fresh white bread when making this dessert.

PREPARATION   30 minutes

BAKING TIME   25 minutes

INGREDIENTS
For 4 to 6 servings
7 ounces (200 g) fresh white bread
Butter for bread
2¼ pounds (1 kg) tart cooking apples
⅔ cup (150 g) granulated sugar
1 vanilla bean
1 lemon peel, finely chopped [optional]
2 cups (½ l) apricot sauce (Recipe 14) *or* vanilla sauce
  (Recipe 12)
Confectioners' sugar

UTENSILS
Straight-sided charlotte mold 6¼″ (16 cm)
Saucepan
Electric mixer

Assembling the Charlotte: Slice the bread into thin slices; butter one side of each slice. Toast the buttered sides under the broiler. Cut each slice into a rectangle 3″ by 1¼″ (8 cm × 3 cm). Line the mold with the slices of bread (the buttered side against the mold), overlapping the slices.

Preheat the oven to 450°F (240°C).

Peel, core, and quarter the apples. Prepare an apple sauce by stewing the apples with the sugar and the vanilla bean until they are soft (the lemon peel can be added if the apples are too sweet). Pass the softened apples through a sieve to make apple sauce. Fill the mold with the apple sauce.

Baking: Bake in 450°F (240°C) oven for about 10 minutes, then lower the heat to 425°F (220°C) and bake for 15 minutes more. Cool the charlotte before turning it out. Cover the top of the charlotte with an apricot sauce or a vanilla sauce. Sprinkle the sides with confectioners' sugar and serve.

Bread and Butter Pudding

PREPARATION	20 minutes
BAKING TIME	30 minutes
INGREDIENTS	*For 6 servings* 7 ounces (200 g) fresh sandwich bread, uncut Butter for bread 2 cups, generous (½ l), milk 1 vanilla bean 3 eggs 2 egg yolks ½ cup, generous (125 g), granulated sugar
UTENSILS	Wire whisk Mixing bowl Oval baking dish 13″ (32 cm) long Baking dish large enough to contain oval baking dish Spoon Knife

Preparing and Baking: Remove the crust from the bread and slice very thin. Lightly butter these slices and cut them in half, from corner to corner, so that each piece forms 2 triangles. Brown the buttered side under the broiler for about 3 minutes. Cover the bottom of the oval baking dish with the bread, toasted side up in overlapping pieces.

Preheat the oven to 425°F (220°C). Boil the milk with the vanilla bean. Beat the eggs and the egg yolks with the sugar for a few minutes until the mixture whitens. Then, slowly pour the hot milk (not boiling) into the egg mixture, stirring all the while. Pour the mixture carefully over the bread, holding the bread slices in place with a spatula, so that they will not float up. Place the smaller baking dish into the large one; pour boiling water into the large dish until it comes halfway up the side of the smaller dish. Bake for 30 minutes in a 425°F (220°C) oven. In the beginning, push down the slices of bread that rise to the surface. When baked, remove from the oven and allow to cool, then refrigerate the pudding until ready to serve.

This pudding can be served with vanilla sauce (Recipe 12) or a raspberry sauce (Recipe 14).

Tropical Fruit Salad

This recipe is given here as a supplement to the other fruit recipes. The comments made about tropical fruits may sometimes be of interest for sherbet making or when using these fruits in other desserts. The following is, in fact, not really a recipe, but more a general outline of a procedure you can adapt to make your own tropical fruit salads. The amounts of the tropical fruits are not given, since this is up to you and to the availability of these fruits in your area. Tropical fruits can be used exclusively to make the salad or in combination with other more common fruits, depending on your taste. In general, allow about 4 to 5 ounces (125 to 150 g) of combined ingredients per serving (i. e., a pound of prepared fruit plus sugar will serve four).

Prepare the basic fruit sauce and add the fruits of your choice to it; it is preferable to make the salad a day in advance and leave to macerate overnight before serving. Some fruits, like bananas and kiwis, being used for decoration, should be added to the salad only at the last minute. In general, two or three tropical fruits mixed with the basic fruit sauce make a varied and delicious salad; the quantity and variety of the fruit employed depends on your taste.

INGREDIENTS

For Basic Fruit Sauce for a salad serving 10 to 12
A 1-quart (1-*l*) jar of apricots in light syrup
1 pineapple weighing approximately 2¼ pounds (1 kg)
4 medium oranges
½ cup (100 g) granulated cane sugar

UTENSILS

Electric blender
Mixing bowl
Knife

Tropical Fruit Salad, Recipe 96
1. *Limes*
2. *Yellow Passion Fruit*
3. *Red Bananas*
4. *Mangosteens*
5. *Rambutans*
6. *Mangos*
7. *Guavas*
8. *Brown Passion Fruit*
9. *Pineapples*
10. *Kiwis*

Making the Basic Fruit Sauce: Drain the apricots and place them with a little of their syrup in the blender and blend until smooth. This apricot puree will be the basis of your fruit sauce. Pour the puree into a bowl.

Peel the pineapple and squeeze the juice in the pineapple skin into the bowl with the apricot puree; core the pineapple and slice it; then cut the slices into small wedges and add them to the bowl of puree as well.

Wash the oranges, cut off and discard the two ends of each orange, but do not peel them. Slice each orange very thinly; then cut each slice into quarters. Place the pieces of orange into a bowl with the cane sugar and leave overnight before mixing them with the apricot–pineapple mixture.

The Tropical Fruits: See the introductory comments on choice and amounts of tropical fruits to use in the salad. (See photo to help identify the fruits themselves.)

Guava: The guava is first green, then it turns yellow with slightly reddish marbling when ripe. It is a flavorful fruit and slightly acid. Peel the fruit as you would an apple and then slice it into the salad; add a little nutmeg to the salad at the same time.

Kiwi: This small oval fruit has a soft, peach-like, brown exterior but is bright green with brilliant, black seeds inside. It is very rich in vitamin C and is ripe when soft to the touch. It can be eaten by cutting it in half and scooping out the pulp or peeled and cut into slices. When sliced, it is added to the basic fruit sauce given earlier; a few slices should be placed on top of the salad at the last minute to decorate.

Kumquat: This is a familiar fruit to many people but an exotic treat to others. Kumquats are orange-like fruits about the size of an olive, which are generally eaten whole, skin and all. Fresh kumquats should be cut in half and left to soak in a bowl with a little white rum for 30 minutes before adding them to the salad. Canned kumquats in thick syrup can be used, in which case they are drained, cut in half, and added directly to the other ingredients used to make the salad (some of their syrup can be added to the salad if the fruit sauce seems too acid).

Limes: Limes, which are a nice addition to punches and can be used to make sherbet, are squeezed like lemons. Their juice is added to the basic fruit sauce described above.

Litchi or Leechi: Litchis are generally small, about the size of a strawberry, with reddish-brown, hard, exterior skins. Once the skin is peeled off, the fruit itself is soft and white with a smooth, brown seed in its center. Only the white pulp is eaten. Place the peeled litchis in a bowl with a little white rum for 30 minutes before adding them to the fruit salad. If canned litchis are used, simply drain them and cut them in half over the salad bowl.

Mango: Mangos, which generally weigh from ½ pound (250 g) to 1 pound 5 ounces (600 g), vary in color depending on the variety employed. They are often apricot-yellow and are soft to the touch when ripe. If purchased unripe, they should be left at room temperature (not refrigerated) to ripen. To use, peel off the skin and cut the pulp surrounding the central pit into small cubes.

Mangosteen: Not to be confused with mangos, the mangosteen is reddish-brown outside and soft to the touch when ripe. It is peeled and eaten much like a tangerine or cut open with a knife to expose the sweet whitish pulp which can be added to the other fruits used in making tropical fruit salad.

Papaya: Papayas are the size and shape of a somewhat elongated melon. Some varieties are green when ripe but most turn yellow or orange. The fruit is peeled and sliced, and when added to a tropical fruit salad, add a little port or lemon juice at the same time to highlight the fruit's taste.

Passion Fruit: There are two common varieties of this fruit; one with a reddish skin and one with a yellow skin. The reddish variety is the more flavorful of the two, although they can be used interchangeably. The fruit is generally about the size of a lemon, and the skin becomes wrinkled and indented all over when the fruit is ripe. Passion fruit can be stored at room temperature to ripen if not purchased ripe. When ripe, cut the fruit in half and scoop out the very soft pulp, which is filled with seeds; this pulp, seeds and all, can be eaten as it is, or it can be worked through a sieve to eliminate the seeds, as when making sherbets (Recipe 100).

For salads, work the pulp through a sieve as well, and mix the strained juice with an equal amount of cane sugar. The resulting passion fruit sauce can be used instead of the basic fruit sauce given initially or simply added to the basic fruit sauce when making tropical fruit salads.

Rambutan: When peeled, this fruit looks almost identical to a litchi, but when still in its skin, it is easily distinguishable because of the soft, hair-like protrusions that cover its exterior. The fruit is peeled and used like litchis.

Red Banana: Generally smaller and firmer than ordinary bananas, red bananas should be firm but never hard when used in salads. To use them, simply peel and slice them as you would any other banana, adding them to the salad just before serving.

To Serve: Tropical fruit salad can be served in a variety of unusual and decorative ways. A pineapple or melon (a watermelon can be used if serving a large party) can be cut in half and hollowed out; then filled with the fruit salad to serve. The pulp of the pineapple or melon is added to the salad before serving. The salad can also be served in seashells, champagne glasses, in individual bowls or in a large serving bowl as shown in the photo.

Choosing and Using an Ice Cream Freezer

There are basically two types of freezers: those that are placed in a deep freezer to chill the cream; and those that rely on a mixture of ice and salt to freeze it. To make the recipes in this book, you will need a 2-quart ice-and-salt freezer, so always have plenty of ice on hand.

Prepare the ice cream or sherbet mixture as described in the recipes and chill it thoroughly before beginning to freeze it; a warm mixture will melt the ice before the ice cream or sherbet is ready. Place the mixture in the canister and place the ice around it in 3 to 4 layers, with about 3 handfuls of salt (preferably coarse or kosher salt) sprinkled over each layer. The ice should come up to the top edge of the canister.

In general, ice creams and sherbets take from 20 to 40 minutes to freeze. When ready, the mixture should still be smooth and creamy, but stiff enough to have begun piling up and clinging to the dasher. The ice cream or sherbet can be served as it comes from the freezer, but it is generally preferable to make it in advance, place it in a mold, and place it in a deep freezer to stiffen a bit more before serving.

Storing and Serving

Keep the mold in the deep freezer while the ice cream or sherbet is being made, then place it in the mold as soon as it is ready. Molds are made of various metals or plastic, and the square shape is most common. Label the ice cream with the date made, the flavor, and the quantity, cover, and store at a temperature of 0°F (–18°C) or lower. Ice creams may be stored for up to 3 weeks, but sherbets should be served no more than 2 weeks after being made.

To serve in scoops, take the mold from the freezer and place it in the refrigerator for 20 to 40 minutes before serving to soften. Test from time to time; when a knife blade penetrates the ice cream or sherbet easily, it is soft enough to serve. If it starts becoming too soft before you can serve it, simply place it back in the freezer.

To unmold a frozen dessert onto a platter, dip the mold in a large bowl of lukewarm water at least ½ hour before you intend to place it in the refrigerator to soften. The water should come all the way up the sides of the mold but not over the edge. If using a plastic mold, hold it in the water for about 5 seconds, lift out, and wipe dry. Turn it upside down over the platter, and pull on opposite sides while pressing on the bottom with your thumbs. If using a metal mold, hold it in the water for 10 seconds, wipe dry, and run the blade of a knife all around the inside edge, with the tip of the knife touching the bottom of the mold. Turn the mold on its side, give a few whacks on the side facing up, then rapidly turn it upside down over the platter, shaking it in little jerks to make the dessert slide out.

Once the dessert is on the platter, place it back in the deep freezer for 30 minutes so that the outside, which will have started to melt, can harden again. Before serving, place in the refrigerator and test for softness as described (any holes made with the knife can be smoothed over with the back of a spoon).

172

97

28° Sugar Syrup for Sherbet

This syrup, used in all sherbets, is called "28° sugar syrup," referring to its density on the Baumé scale (see Note). The technicalities need not concern most readers; what is important is to follow the instructions to the letter.

PREPARATION   5 minutes

INGREDIENTS   *For 6⅔ cups (1½ l) of 28° Sugar Syrup*
                     5 cups (1 kg) granulated sugar
                     4¼ cups (1 *l*) water

UTENSILS   Large saucepan
                     Wooden spoon
                     Large bowl or jar

Making the Syrup: Place the water and sugar in a large saucepan. Place over high heat, stirring with a wooden spoon until the sugar has dissolved. Continue heating until the syrup comes to a full boil. Then immediately remove the saucepan from the heat and pour the syrup into a large bowl or the jar in which you wish to store it. Leave to cool completely before using.

To Store: Once the syrup has cooled completely, cover the jar in which it is to be stored and place it in the refrigerator. This sugar syrup keeps for months, and it is always a good idea to have a jar of it in the refrigerator ready.

Note: The density of this syrup is very important; what is generally called a "light" syrup is one with a low density, while a "heavy" syrup is one with a high density. When cooking sugar, a candy thermometer is used to measure the temperature, but when density is involved, measurements are made on a simple instrument called a *hydrometer*. A hydrometer is about the size and shape of an ordinary medical thermometer, but it is a bit longer and has an enlarged, weighted end. To use this instrument, the sugar syrup in question is poured into a small narrow beaker and the hydrometer is lowered gently into the syrup. The hydrometer is graduated on its stem with the various densities; once in the syrup, the density is read at the point the floatation line crosses the hydrometer. For years, density was expressed in Baumé degrees, but hydrometers have recently switched to a decimal density system, even though the Baumé degrees are still often referred to. The sugar syrup used in making sherbets in this book is consistently referred to as a 28° sugar syrup, although its density could also be expressed as 1.241 on the modern decimal scale. Since only one sugar syrup is used in this book, you do not need a hydrometer when making it. The recipe is accurate and simple enough so that a 28° sugar syrup is automatically produced if it is followed scrupulously.

173

98

Apricot Sherbet

PREPARATION	5 to 15 minutes
FREEZING TIME	20 to 40 minutes
INGREDIENTS	*For approximately 1 quart (1 l) of sherbet* *Using fresh apricots:* Generous 1⅔ cup (4 d*l*) 28° Sugar Syrup (Recipe 97) 4 cups (500 g) pitted fresh apricot halves *Using canned apricots:* 1½ quart (1½ *l*) can or jar of pitted apricot halves in light syrup Generous ¾ cup (2 d*l*) cold 28° Sugar Syrup (Recipe 97)
UTENSILS	Colander (optional) Electric blender Ice cream freezer Mold

Making the Sherbet: *Using fresh apricots:* Heat the sugar syrup in a saucepan, add the apricots, and simmer for 10 minutes; the liquid must not boil. Pour the contents of the saucepan into an electric blender and blend until smooth. Pour into a bowl and leave the mixture to cool completely; to speed chilling, stand the bowl containing the apricot puree in another bowl filled with ice and water. Stir constantly and renew the ice water when necessary.

Using canned apricots: Drain the fruit. Place 2½ cups (500 g) of the drained fruit in a blender and blend until smooth; there should be 2 generous cups (5 d*l*) of puree after blending. (The extra apricot halves may be used to decorate the top and sides of the finished sherbet). Stir the sugar syrup into the apricot puree, and chill for 1 hour.

To Freeze: When the apricot mixture is perfectly cold, pour it into the ice cream freezer. Then freeze, mold, and serve.

99

Raspberry Sherbet

PREPARATION	10 minutes
FREEZING TIME	20 to 40 minutes
INGREDIENTS	*For approximately 1 quart (1 l) of sherbet* 2¼ pints (550 g) fresh raspberries (see Comment) Scant 2 cups (4.5 dl) cold 28° Sugar Syrup (Recipe 97)
UTENSILS	Electric blender Bowl Spoon Ice cream freezer Mold

Making the Sherbet: Place the raspberries in a blender and blend to make a puree; you need 2 generous cups (5 dl) of puree for making the sherbet. Mix the puree with the sugar syrup and pour into the ice cream freezer; then mold and serve.

Serving Suggestions: Raspberry Sherbet can be molded to make combination desserts with vanilla ice cream or champagne sherbet. It is also used in making the Frozen Raspberry Vacherin (Recipe 119) and the Raspberry Tulip (Recipe 116).

Comment: Frozen raspberry puree can be used instead of fresh raspberries. Do *not* allow it to thaw. Take it from the freezer and place it directly in a blender with the sugar syrup. When blended, pour into the ice cream freezer and freeze. Freezing time will be slightly shorter using frozen fruit puree.

100

Passion Fruit Sherbet

PREPARATION	20 minutes
FREEZING TIME	20 to 40 minutes
INGREDIENTS	*For approximately 1 quart (1 l) of sherbet* 2¼ pounds (1 kg) Passion Fruit (see Comment) 2 generous cups (½ l) cold 28° Sugar Syrup (Recipe 97) 1 generous cup (¼ l) noneffervescent mineral water
UTENSILS	Serrated knife Spoon Food mill, drum sieve, *or* electric juicer Sieve Mixing bowl Spoon Ice cream freezer Mold

Making the Sherbet: Cut each fruit in half and scoop out all the pulp and seeds with a spoon. Either run the pulp through an electric juicer or work it through a food mill or drum sieve and strain out any bits of seed through a sieve. The strained pulp and juice from the fruit should measure 1 generous cup (¼ l). Pour this into a bowl and mix it with the sugar syrup and water. Then pour it into the ice cream freezer, freeze, mold, and serve

Serving Suggestions: Passion Fruit Sherbet can be molded and served with Coconut Ice Cream (see Recipe 106) or simply scooped and served garnished with slices of fresh kiwi fruit.

Comment: The best passion fruits are those with red pulp; those with yellow pulp tend to be slightly more acid, although either can be used for this recipe. Do not be put off by the shriveled appearance of the fruit—this is a sign that it is perfectly ripe.

101

Banana Sherbet

PREPARATION	10 minutes
FREEZING TIME	20 to 40 minutes
INGREDIENTS	*For approximately 1 quart (1 l) of sherbet* 1 pound 10½ ounces (750 g) bananas (4 to 6 bananas, depending on size) Scant 1⅓ cups (3 d*l*) cold 28° Sugar Syrup (Recipe 97) Juice of ½ lemon Generous ¾ cup (2 d*l*) noneffervescent mineral water 2 teaspoons rum (preferably white)
UTENSILS	Food mill *or* food processor Large mixing bowl Spoon Ice cream freezer Mold

Making the Sherbet: Peel the bananas and grind them through a food mill or puree them in a food processor to make a smooth puree. Do not use an electric blender because it will make the puree too foamy and sticky. Measure the puree; you need a generous 1⅔ cups (4 d*l*) for making the sherbet.

In a large bowl, mix the puree with the cold sugar syrup, lemon juice, mineral water, and rum. Then pour into the ice cream freezer and freeze until ready, then mold and serve

Serving Suggestions: Serve banana sherbet with hot Chocolate Sauce (Recipe 13).

Banana sherbet can be used to make numerous combination desserts; it can be molded and served with Coconut Ice Cream (Recipe 106) or Chocolate Ice Cream (Recipe 104).

102
Champagne Sherbet

PREPARATION	10 minutes
FREEZING TIME	20 to 40 minutes
INGREDIENTS	*For approximately 1 quart (1 l) of sherbet* Generous 1⅔ cups (4 dl) champagne (see Comment) Generous 1⅔ cup (4 dl) cold 28° Sugar Syrup (Recipe 97) ⅔ cup (1.5 dl) noneffervescent mineral water Juice of 1 lemon or ½ orange
UTENSILS	Ice cream freezer Mold

Making the Sherbet: Place all the ingredients listed in the ice cream freezer; they will mix together as the sherbet is being frozen. Then freeze, mold, and serve.

Serving Suggestions: Mold with Raspberry Sherbet (Recipe 99).

Comment: Use a very good, full-bodied champagne for making this sherbet (preferably a pink champagne from a vintage year). All sherbets made with alcohol are very fragile; they should not be saved, but always served the day they are made.

103

Vanilla Ice Cream

PREPARATION	15 to 20 minutes
COOKING TIME	Approximately 10 minutes for cooking the cream
COOLING TIME	Approximately 30 minutes on ice before freezing
FREEZING TIME	20 to 40 minutes
INGREDIENTS	*For approximately 1 quart (1 l) of ice cream* 2 generous cups (½ *l*) milk 1 vanilla bean split open lengthwise 1 generous cup (210 g) granulated sugar 6 egg yolks 1 generous cup (¼ *l*) heavy cream or crème fraîche
UTENSILS	1 medium-sized saucepan with cover 2 mixing bowls Electric mixer *or* wire whisk Wooden spoon *or* spatula Candy thermometer (optional) Ice cream freezer Molds

Sweetening and Flavoring the Milk: Place the milk, vanilla bean, and half the sugar in a sauce pan and bring to a boil. Once the milk boils, cover the pot and remove from the heat. Let the mixture stand for 10 minutes before proceeding with the recipe.

Note 1:   In many other ice creams the flavoring is not added to the milk at this stage. When the flavoring (i.e., chocolate, fruit puree, etc.) is added later—generally after the cream has been cooked—the milk and half of the sugar must still be brought to a boil to dissolve the sugar but need not be left to stand before proceeding with the recipe.

Preparing the Egg Yolk–Sugar Mixture: Place the egg yolks and remaining sugar in a bowl and beat with an electric mixer or wire whisk until the mixture whitens and forms a ribbon.

Making the Cream: Place the saucepan containing the milk, vanilla bean, and sugar over high heat and bring back to a boil. Pour a little of the boiling milk into

179

the bowl with the egg yolk–sugar mixture, whisking constantly as the liquid is added. Remove the saucepan of milk from the heat and pour the contents of the bowl into it, stirring constantly with a wooden spoon or spatula.

Cooking the Cream: Place the saucepan back over low heat, using a candy thermometer to watch the temperature of the cream as it cooks. Stir the cream constantly—it should never be allowed to boil. As it cooks, the cream will thicken perceptibly, especially toward the end of the cooking time. If using a candy thermometer, cook the cream until the thermometer registers 185°F (85°C), then remove from the heat and continue stirring for 1 to 2 minutes more before cooling the cream.

Although it is preferable to use a candy thermometer when cooking the cream, it is not absolutely necessary. As the cream cooks and thickens, it will begin to lightly coat the wooden spatula used to stir it. Lift the spatula periodically out of the cream and hold it at a tilt so that the excess cream will fall from the spatula back into the saucepan. Use your finger to draw a line in the thin film of cream that adheres to the spatula. If the cream needs to be cooked longer, the line will quickly lose its shape and the cream on the spatula will look as thin as milk. When sufficiently cooked, the cream will nicely coat the spatula and the top edge of the line will hold its shape. When the cream is cooked, it should immediately be removed from the heat.

Cooking the cream generally takes about 5 to 10 minutes (see Comment).

Cooling the Cream: Once the cream is cooked, lift out the vanilla bean and pour the cream into a bowl. Add the crème fraîche or heavy cream to the bowl, stirring constantly to mix well (see Note 2). The addition of the chilled cream both enriches and starts cooling the cooked ingredients. The finished cream must now be allowed to cool *completely* before being placed in the ice cream freezer. To speed cooling, place the bowl containing the cream in a slightly larger bowl that has previously been filled with ice cubes and water. Stir the cream frequently as it cools, and test the temperature using your finger. The cream should feel cold to the touch when finished cooling, which takes about 30 minutes in ice water.

Note 2:   Not all ice creams in this book add chilled crème fraîche or heavy cream to the cooked ingredients. Cooking and cooling instructions apply to all ice creams with or without the addition of chilled cream at this stage of the preparation. If whipped cream is called for, it is always folded in after the cooked cream has cooled completely.

To Freeze the Cream: Once the cream is completely cold, pour it into the ice cream freezer and start the machine. Then freeze, mold, and serve (see pages 2 to 6).

Comment: Great care must be taken when cooking the cream. If heated too much, the egg will curdle and the cream will look grainy. If this happens, remove the saucepan from the heat, take out the vanilla bean, immediately add 1 tablespoon of cold milk or cream to the pot, and pour the cream into an electric blender. Blend until smooth; then proceed as described under the heading "Cooling the Cream."

To Freeze the Cream: Once the cream is completely cold, pour it into the ice cream freezer and start the machine. Then freeze, mold, and serve.

Serving Suggestions: The wonderfully subtle taste of Vanilla Ice Cream makes it the perfect partner to various other flavors when making molded desserts. It can be served alone or with a scoop of Chocolate Ice Cream (Recipe 104), Coffee Ice Cream (Recipe 105), or Raspberry Sherbet (Recipe 99). It can also be served simply topped with a Fresh Fruit Sauce (Recipe 14) or hot Chocolate Sauce (Recipe 13).

To Store: This ice cream may be stored in the freezer for 2 weeks.

104

Chocolate Ice Cream

PREPARATION	10 minutes
COOKING TIME	Approximately 10 minutes for the cream
COOLING TIME	Approximately 30 minutes on ice before freezing
FREEZING TIME	20 to 40 minutes
INGREDIENTS	*For approximately 1 quart (1 l) of ice cream* Scant 3¼ cups (¾ l) milk 1 generous cup (210 g) granulated sugar 6 egg yolks 6 tablespoons (60 g) cocoa powder
UTENSILS	1 medium-sized saucepan with cover 3 mixing bowls Electric mixer *or* wire whisk Ice cream freezer Wooden spoon *or* spatula Molds Candy thermometer (optional)

Making the Ice Cream: Using the milk, sugar, and egg yolks, make and cook the cream as described in Recipe 103 for Vanilla Ice Cream.

Once the cream is cooked but before it is allowed to cool, place the cocoa powder in a bowl and whisk in the hot cream, a tablespoon at a time at the beginning; more cooked cream can be progressively added to the cocoa each time. Whisk constantly until all the cream has been added and a smooth mixture has been formed. Cool the cream as described in Recipe 103. Pour the mixture into the ice cream freezer and freeze, then mold and serve.

105

Coffee Ice Cream

PREPARATION	20 minutes
COOKING TIME	Approximately 10 minutes for the cream
COOLING TIME	Approximately 30 minutes on ice before freezing
FREEZING TIME	20 to 40 minutes

INGREDIENTS

For approximately 1 quart (1 l) of ice cream
Generous ½ cup (50 g) coarsely ground coffee beans
2 generous cups (½ l) milk
1 generous cup (210 g) granulated sugar
6 egg yolks
1 generous cup (¼ l) heavy cream or crème fraîche
20 sugar coffee beans (optional)

UTENSILS

2 medium saucepans	Wooden spoon *or* spatula
1 cover for saucepan	Candy thermometer
2 mixing bowls	(optional)
Fine sieve	Ice cream freezer
Electric mixer *or* wire whisk	Molds

Making the Ice Cream: Place the ground coffee in a saucepan with the milk and half of the sugar. Stir and bring to a boil, then cover and remove the pot from the heat. Let the ingredients stand for 10 minutes. Then pour the contents of the saucepan through a fine sieve into another saucepan.

Combine these ingredients with the other half of the sugar, the egg yolks, and the heavy cream; finish making, cooking, and cooling the cream as described in Recipe 103 for Vanilla Ice Cream. Pour the finished, chilled cream into an ice cream freezer and freeze.

To Mold: Coffee Ice Cream should be molded and covered as soon as it comes from the ice cream freezer since it has a tendency to discolor when exposed to the air.

If desired, sugar coffee beans can be stirred into the ice cream just before it is molded and stored.

106
Coconut Ice Cream

PREPARATION	20 minutes
COOKING TIME	Approximately 10 minutes for the cream
COOLING TIME	Approximately 30 minutes on ice before freezing
FREEZING TIME	20 to 40 minutes
INGREDIENTS	*For approximately 1 quart (1 l) of ice cream* 2 generous cups (½ l) milk 1 cup (75 g) grated coconut 1 generous cup (210 g) granulated sugar 6 egg yolks 1 generous cup (¼ l) heavy cream or creme fraîche
UTENSILS	1 medium-sized saucepan with cover 2 mixing bowls Electric mixer *or* wire whisk Wooden spoon *or* spatula Candy thermometer (optional) Ice cream freezer Molds

Making the Ice Cream: Using these ingredients, make the ice cream following Recipe 103 for making Vanilla Ice Cream. All of the coconut should be added to the milk in the beginning and allowed to stand. Do *not* strain the milk before combining it with the egg yolk–sugar mixture, since it is pleasant to have the grated coconut in the finished ice cream.

Serving Suggestions: Serve scoops of Coconut Ice Cream in a coconut shell that has been emptied of its milk and split in half—do not remove the pulp from the coconut shell. **Decorate with a Chocolate Palm (Recipe 21).**

Coconut Ice Cream can be molded to make combination desserts with Passion Fruit Sherbet (Recipe 100) or Banana Sherbet (Recipe 101).

This ice cream can also be served simply with Fresh Pineapple Sauce (Recipe 14) and coconut cookies.

GENERAL COMMENTS ON SUNDAES

Sundaes are desserts made with scoops of one or more flavors or ice cream or sherbet. Sundaes are always served with a sauce and are often served with small pieces of fruit, pastry, or meringue to garnish them. The ice cream or sherbet used in making a sundae can be prepared hours, even days, in advance but the sauce and garnishing elements are added only at the last minute.

Included with the sundaes are several desserts served in cup-like pastry shells called tulip pastries (*tulipes* in French). The pastry here replaces the glass in these sundae-like desserts (see photo, page 195).

Most of the sundaes in this book are small, delicately arranged, and subtly flavored. Unlike American versions of this type of dessert, French sundaes are often composed of only a few elements, many times using a sauce the same flavor as the ice cream or sherbet to intensify the taste experience.

One quart (1 *l*) of ice cream or sherbet will make about 20 scoops if using an ice cream scoop of a 3-tablespoon (5-c*l*) capacity, which is the size I suggest using. When you have to prepare a lot of sundaes, it is convenient to scoop the ice cream being used a day ahead of time and freeze the scoops as follows. Remove the stored ice cream or sherbet from the freezer and place it in the refrigerator to soften as described on page 172. Place a piece of nonstick parchment paper on a large plate in the freezer and turn the freezer down to its lowest setting. Leave the plate in the freezer for at least 15 minutes.

When the ice cream has softened enough, remove the plate from the freezer and scoop the ice cream onto the paper. Put the plate back into the freezer, and when the scoops have hardened, place them in a freezer bag or a box that can be tightly closed. In this way, the scoops can be kept in the freezer for up to 10 days. When needed, the scoops should be arranged in the serving dishes or glasses and allowed to thaw in the refrigerator until soft enough to serve in the same way as any stored ice cream.

The following recipes for sundaes are only a sampling of the many desserts that can be made in the same way. Try your skills at combining other ice creams, sherbets, and sauces. Sundaes are generally served either in a tall narrow glass or a wide champagne-style one. Of course, special sundae glasses or any small dish or bowl can be used when making this type dessert. In any case, the receptacle used for the sundae should be placed in the freezer for at least 15 minutes before being filled with the ice cream, sauce, and garnish.

Important: All of the following sundae recipes are for making 1 sundae—that is, 1 serving. By simply multiplying the amounts of the ingredients given with each sundae, you can easily calculate what you need to make 4, 5, 6, or 10 identical sundaes.

♕

107

Coffee Liégeois Sundae

(Photo page 186)

PREPARATION   5 minutes

INGREDIENTS

For 1 serving
2 scoops of Coffee Ice Cream (Recipe 105)
3 tablespoons (½ d*l*) very sweet, cold, black coffee

For decoration
1 generous tablespoon Chantilly Cream (Recipe 1)
3 sugar coffee beans (optional)

Making the Dessert: (See the General Comments on Sundaes.) Place the ice cream in a tall cold glass, pour over the cold, sweetened coffee, and top with a generous spoonful of Chantilly Cream. Sprinkle a few sugar coffee beans over the Chantilly to decorate, and serve immediately.

♕

108

Juanita Banana Sundae

(Photo page 186)

PREPARATION   5 minutes

INGREDIENTS

For 1 serving
2 scoops of Vanilla Ice Cream (Recipe 103)
½ banana (split lengthwise)
3 tablespoons (½ d*l*) hot Chocolate Sauce (Recipe 13)

For decoration
Chantilly Cream (Recipe 1)

Making the Dessert: (See the General Comments on Sundaes.) In a crescent-shaped serving dish (see photo) or on a plate, place the ice cream and the half banana. Spoon over the hot Chocolate Sauce and decorate with a little Chantilly Cream squeezed from a pastry bag to make a rose-like mound. Serve immediately.

As shown in the photo, the chocolate sauce can be put in the serving dish before the other ingredients, if desired.

♛

109
Ivory Coast Sundae
(Photo page 186)

PREPARATION   5 minutes

INGREDIENTS

For 1 serving
1 scoop of Chocolate Ice Cream (Recipe 104)
1 scoop of Banana Sherbet (Recipe 101)
3 tablespoons (½ d*l*) Vanilla Sauce (Recipe 12)

For decoration
1 Chocolate Palm (Recipe 21))

Making the Dessert: (See the General Comments on Sundaes.) Place the scoop of ice cream and the scoop of sherbet next to each other in a cold serving glass or in a previously refrigerated calabash shell. Spoon over the Vanilla Sauce, decorate with the Chocolate Palm, and serve immediately. (The Vanilla Sauce can also be served under the ice cream as shown in the photograph.)

♛

110
Passion Fruit Sundae
(Photo page 188)

PREPARATION   5 minutes

INGREDIENTS

For 1 serving
1 scoop of Coconut Ice Cream (Recipe 106)
1 scoop of Passion Fruit Sherbet (Recipe 100)
½ a coconut or ½ a calabash
3 tablespoons (½ d*l*) Vanilla Sauce (Recipe 12)

For decoration
Chocolate Palm (Recipe 21—optional)

Making the Dessert: (See the General Comments on Sundaes.) Place a scoop of ice cream and a scoop of sherbet in the half coconut or calabash, spoon over the vanilla sauce, decorate with the chocolate palm, and serve immediately.

$$\text{♕ ♕}$$

111

Sherbet-Filled Fruits

This recipe is for oranges, tangerines, lemons, and grapefruits.

PREPARATION	30 minutes
COOLING TIME	1 hour

INGREDIENTS	*For 8 servings*
	8 oranges
	   or 16 tangerines
	   or 8 large lemons
	   or 4 grapefruits
	Sugar cubes
	1 quart (1 *l*) of sherbet made from the juice of the fruit
	   employed or made in advance with other fruit
	
	For decoration (optional)
	Green Almond Paste leaves (Recipe 19)
	Candied cherries

UTENSILS	Sharp knife Lemon or orange squeezer Spoon or pastry bag with a star-shaped nozzle (optional)

General Comments: Sherbet used for filling citrus fruit skins can be prepared well in advance but must be softened to a "newly made" consistency before use.

The hollowed-out skin may be frozen and kept in the freezer for up to 4 days before being filled with the sherbet. Once the sherbet has been placed in the skin, however, the dessert should be served within 12 hours or the skin will impart a bitter taste to the sherbet.

For these desserts, always select somewhat thick-skinned fruit (nontreated, if possible). Wash and dry the fruit well before scooping out the pulp and freezing the skins.

Making Sherbet-Filled Fruits: (See Note). Cut off the tops of the lemons, oranges, or tangerines two-thirds up from the bottom; grapefruits are cut in half. Using a lemon or orange squeezer, squeeze the fruit carefully to get the maximum amount of juice without damaging the peel. Use the juice to make the sherbet if it has not been prepared in advance.

Remove the thin membranes that fill the center and are attached to the insides of the peel; then rub the inside of each peel with a sugar cube. Do the same with the top part of each fruit. Make sure the hollowed-out bottom peel will stand upright—if not, cut a thin slice off the base to make it flat and stable. Place the hollowed-out bottoms and tops in the freezer for at least an hour before filling them with sherbet.

Fill each peel, either using a spoon or (if the sherbet is soft enough) a pastry bag. Cover the sherbet with the top of the fruit except in the case of grapefruits, in which case each half is simply filled with sherbet (see photo). Place the dessert immediately back in the freezer until ready to serve. Serve within 12 hours. (see General Comments on Serving Ice Cream, Sherbet, etc., pages 5 to 7).

Note: All sherbet-filled fruits are made in the same way; they differ only in that you should serve two tangerines, one orange or lemon, and half a grapefruit per person.

The finished desserts may be decorated either with little leaves made of green almond paste or with candied cherries, or served simply as they are (see photo).

♜

112

Champagne and Raspberry Sundae

PREPARATION   **5 minutes**

INGREDIENTS   *For 1 serving*
2 scoops of Raspberry Sherbet (Recipe 99)
1 scoop of Champagne Sherbet (Recipe 102)
3 tablespoons (½ d*l*) Fresh Raspberry Sauce (Recipe 14)

For decoration
A few candied pineapple slices
Fresh raspberries

Making the Dessert: (See the General Comments on Sundaes.) Place the scoops of sherbert on top of each other in a tall cold glass, spoon over the fresh raspberry sauce, and decorate with the candied pineapple slices and fresh raspberries. Serve immediately.

113

Vanilla Wafer Batter

PREPARATION   15 minutes

SOFTENING TIME   2 hours

INGREDIENTS   *For approximately 1½ cups (400 g) of batter that make*
16 tulip pastries or 80 wafers
7 tablespoons (110 g) butter
⅔ cup (130 g) granulated sugar
4 egg whites = ⅔ cup (130 g)
1 vanilla bean *or* 4 drops vanilla extract
1 scant cup (130 g) flour

UTENSILS

Knife	Large mixing bowl
Small mixing bowl	Electric mixer *or* wire whisk
Saucepan *or* double boiler	Wooden spatula
Yoghurt thermometer (optional)	Sifter

Making the Batter: Take the butter and egg whites from the refrigerator and leave at room temperature for 2 hours before proceeding with the recipe.

Split open the vanilla bean lengthwise and, using the tip of a knife, scrape the dark "filling" out of it and into a bowl containing the sugar; if using the vanilla extract, simply add the extract to the sugar.

Place the egg whites in a bowl or the top of a double boiler; then place some hot (not boiling) water in a saucepan into which the bowl will fit or in the bottom of a double boiler. The bottom of the bowl should not touch the water, which should be very hot, but not burning to the touch [it should register no more than 122°F (50°C) on a yoghurt thermometer]. Allow the egg whites to warm

Rinse a mixing bowl out with very hot water and wipe it dry. Place the softened butter in the bowl and beat it with an electric mixer or a wooden spoon until it is creamy. Add the sugar–vanilla mixture to the butter, beating constantly but slowly; then start adding the warmed egg whites a tablespoon at a time (if working by hand, begin beating the mixture with a wire whisk when adding the egg whites). When the egg whites have been added and the batter is perfectly homogenous, stop beating and sift the flour into the bowl, cutting and stirring it into the other ingredients with a wooden spatula (work quickly but gently when mixing in the flour).

The batter is now ready for use. If not used immediately, it can be kept in the refrigerator for several hours, but it should be used the day it is made.

114

Tulip Pastries

PREPARATION	30 minutes
BAKING TIME	10 minutes
INGREDIENTS	*For 16 tulip pastries* 1½ cups (400 g) Vanilla Wafer Batter (Recipe 113)
UTENSILS	1 circular or square piece of stiff cardboard 8 inches (20 cm) wide (see Note) Tape measure Compass *or* 6-inch (15-cm) wide plate Scissors Nonstick parchment paper (optional) Flexible-blade, metal spatula Baking sheet 8 small mixing bowls *or* 4 small brioche molds with a 1-cup (¼ *l*) capacity

Baking and Shaping the Tulip Pastries: Preheat the oven to 350°F (175°C).

Take a flat cardboard circle or square 8 inches (20 cm) across and draw a smaller circle in the center of it that is only 6 inches (15 cm) wide using a compass or a small plate. With a pair of scissors, cut out this circle and discard. Place the cardboard [now with a 6-inch (15-cm) hole in the middle] in one corner of a baking sheet which has either been lined with a sheet of parchment paper or buttered and lightly floured.

Fill the hollow center of the cardboard with a tablespoon of wafer batter, spreading the batter out with a spatula so that it fills the central circle completely and evenly. Once this is done, carefully lift the cardboard from around the batter and repeat this operation, placing the cardboard successively in each corner of the baking sheet, filling the center and lifting off the "mold" until there are 4 very thin circles of batter on the baking sheet ready to bake. Place the baking sheet in the oven and bake for 10 minutes; when the edges of each baked disk have colored, but the center is still a cream color, the circles are done.

Molding the Batter: Once the batter has been baked, it must be removed from the oven and molded *immediately*. There are two ways of doing this.

Method 1:   Take 8 small mixing bowls all the same size and place 4 of them upside down on a table. As soon as the batter is baked, take the baking sheet from the oven and, using a flexible-blade spatula, lift off the baked circles of batter. Place each circle on one of the upside down bowls, and immediately cover it with another bowl. This must be done very quickly because as the batter cools it becomes brittle and impossible to shape.

Method 2:   Remove each wafer circle from the baking sheet as soon as it comes from the oven, and place each circle immediately into a small ribbed brioche mold. The baked batter will quickly cool to the shape of the mold into which you have put it. This method makes for a very pretty tulip shape with nice pleats all around it.

To Store: The tulip pastries can be stacked inside each other and kept in a cookie box or cake box for up to 2 weeks. They must be placed in the box as soon as they are completely cool; if left out in the open for even a few hours, they become "stale" and rubbery.

Note: The cardboard backing of a pad of paper or the cardboard with which men's shirts are packed are excellent for making this "mold."

♨ ♨

115

Melba Tulip Cookie Dessert

(Photo page 194)

PREPARATION	5 minutes
INGREDIENTS	*For 1 serving*
	1 Tulip Pastry (Recipe 114)
	2 scoops of Vanilla Ice Cream (Recipe 103)
	A few pieces of fresh or canned fruit
	For decoration
	1 tablespoon red currant jelly
	Slivered almonds

Making the Dessert: (See the General Comments on Sundaes.) Place the tulip pastry on a serving plate, put the ice cream into it, and decorate with fruit. Spoon over the currant jelly, sprinkle with slivered almonds, and serve immediately.

Note: As shown in the photo, Fresh Fruit Sauce (made from the same fruit served around the ice cream) can be used instead of jelly with the dessert.

♟ ♟

116
Raspberry Tulip
(Photo page 194)

PREPARATION   5 minutes

INGREDIENTS   *For 1 serving*
1 Tulip Pastry (Recipe 114)
2 scoops of Raspberry Sherbet (Recipe 99)
3 tablespoons (½ dl) Fresh Raspberry Sauce (Recipe 14)

For decoration
1 small bunch of fresh red currants

Making the Dessert: (See the General Comments on Sundaes.) Place the tulip pastry on a plate and fill with the scoops of sherbet, spoon over the raspberry sauce, and decorate with a bunch of fresh red currants. Serve immediately.

GENERAL COMMENTS ON MOLDED COMBINATION DESSERTS

Ice creams and sherbets used in making molded combination desserts must be of a "newly made" consistency; that is, they should be about the softness of ice cream or sherbet when it comes from the ice cream freezer (see the coffee ice cream pictured in the photo). Ideally, therefore, ice creams or sherbets used in molded desserts should be molded immediately or within 1 or 2 hours of the time they come from the ice cream freezer. If previously frozen, ice cream or sherbet must be softened to this "newly made" consistency before being used as an element in a molded combination dessert. This softening is simply done by removing it from the freezer and placing it in the refrigerator for approximately 45 minutes to 1 hour, or until softened to the proper consistency.

Recipes 117 and 118 are molded in an ice cream mold, but recipe 119 is built up inside a flan ring. For this dessert, use an 8-inch (20 cm) ring with a height of 2 inches (5 cm). Place the ring on a flat, rigid piece of cardboard, a plate, or the bottom of a springform cake pan so that the dessert can be easily handled. To remove the ring after the dessert is frozen, carefully rub it with a sponge that has been dipped into hot water and squeezed dry. Then wipe the ring with a cloth and lift it off very gently. Place the dessert back into the refrigerator to soften for about 20 minutes before serving.

The following desserts are only a sampling of the many that can be made by molding and serving two flavors of ice cream or sherbet in the same mold. Using a little imagination, you can create your own molded combination desserts following the principles outlined here.

♔

117
Molded Raspberry and Champagne Dessert
(Photo page 191)

PREPARATION	15 minutes
COOLING TIME	2 to 3 hours
FREEZING TIME	3 hours before serving
INGREDIENTS	*For a 1-quart (1-l) mold serving 6* ½ quart (½ l) Raspberry Sherbet (Recipe 99) ½ cup (100 g) diced candied pineapple slices ½ quart (½ l) Champagne Sherbet (Recipe 102)
UTENSILS	1-quart (1-l) ice cream mold with cover Flexible-blade, metal spatula or spoon

Preliminary Preparations: Place the mold and cover in the freezer for at least 15 minutes before lining it.

Lining the Mold: Take the mold from the freezer and pour the Raspberry Sherbet into the mold. Work quickly, using a flexible-blade metal spatula or a metal spoon to push the sherbet around and up the sides of the mold. Don't worry about neatness or the fact that the sherbet will not line the mold evenly at this stage; this will be done later.

Place the mold back into the freezer for 30 to 40 minutes, after which time the sherbet will have stiffened enough to allow you to even out the lining of the mold. The sherbet should still be soft enough to push, so that it will cover the sides and bottom of the mold in one equally thick, smooth layer, and cold enough so that once pushed up and smoothed out it will hold its shape. If after this second smoothing the sherbet is still too soft to hold its shape when pushed up the sides, it should be refrigerated for another 30 minutes to an hour and the lining completed at that time.

Filling the Center of the Mold: Once the mold has been lined, place it immediately back into the freezer for 1 hour; then stir the pieces of candied

pineapple into the Champagne Sherbet and fill the center of the mold with this mixture. Place the finished dessert in the freezer for at least 3 hours before turning out and serving.

Note: This dessert does not save well and should be served within 24 hours of the time it is made.

♕

118

Molded Vanilla Desserts

PREPARATION	15 minutes
COOLING TIME	2 to 3 hours
FREEZING TIME	3 hours before serving
INGREDIENTS	*For a 1-quart (1-l) mold serving 6*
	To line the mold ½ quart (½ *l*) Vanilla Ice Cream (Recipe 103)
	To fill the center of the mold ½ quart (¹/₂ *l*) Raspberry Sherbet (Recipe 99) *or* Coffee Ice Cream (Recipe 105)
UTENSILS	1-quart (1-*l*) ice cream mold with cover Flexible-blade, metal spatula or spoon

Preliminary Preparations: Place the mold and cover in the freezer for at least 15 minutes before lining it.

Lining the Mold: Take the mold from the freezer and pour the Vanilla Ice Cream into the mold. Work quickly, using a flexible-blade metal spatula or a metal spoon to push the ice cream around and up the sides of the mold. The ice cream should cover the bottom and the sides of the mold. Don't worry about neatness or the fact that the ice cream will not line the mold evenly at this stage; this will be done later.

Place the mold back into the freezer for 30 to 40 minutes, after which time the ice cream will have stiffened enough to allow you to even out the lining of the mold. The ice cream should still be soft enough to push, so that it will cover the sides and bottom of the mold in one equally thick, smooth layer, and cold enough so that once pushed up and smoothed out it will hold its shape. If after this second smoothing the ice cream is still too soft to hold its shape when pushed up the sides, it should be refrigerated for another 30 minutes to an hour and the lining completed at that time. (The time in the freezer varies depending on the stiffness of the ice cream to start with and the temperature of your freezer.)

Filling the Center of the Mold: Once the mold has been lined (see photo), place it immediately back into the freezer for 1 hour before filling the center with the sherbet or ice cream. Once the mold is filled, it must be left in the freezer for at least 3 hours before turning out and serving.

To Store: In a closed mold, molded combination desserts made with vanilla ice cream may be kept in the freezer for up to 2 weeks.

119

Frozen Strawberry or Raspberry Vacherin

PREPARATION	20 minutes
COOLING TIME	1 hour 20 minutes
FREEZING TIME	3 hours before serving

For 1 dessert serving 10
1 French Meringue (Recipe 79),
    8 inches (20 cm) wide and ¾ inch (2 cm) high
½ quart (½ *l*) Vanilla Ice Cream (Recipe 103)
2½ cups (6 d*l*) Raspberry Sherbet (Recipe 99)

For decoration
2 generous cups (½ *l*) Chantilly Cream
    (Recipe 1)
10 oval meringues (Recipe 79)
24 fresh strawberries *or* 32 fresh raspberries
Generous 1⅔ cups (4 d*l*) Fresh Fruit Sauce made with
    either strawberries or raspberries (Recipe 14)

1 flan ring 8 inches (20 cm) wide and 2 inches (5 cm) high
    or a strip of cardboard 24 × 2 inches (61 × 5 cm)
1 cardboard circle, plate, or bottom of a spring form cake
    pan, 9 inches (23 cm) in diameter
Flexible-blade, metal spatula or spoon
Pastry bag with star-shaped nozzle

Making the Dessert: (See the General Comments on Molded Combination Desserts, page 196). Place the flan ring on a piece of cardboard, a plate, or the bottom of a springform cake pan slightly wider than it is. Put the meringue circle into the ring or make a ring of cardboard to go around it, and place it in the freezer for 20 minutes before filling the ring with the other ingredients.

Remove from the freezer and pour either the vanilla ice cream or the raspberry sherbet into the ring to make the first layer. Smooth the surface with a metal spatula or spoon to cover the meringue evenly, and then place back into the freezer for 1 hour before finishing to fill the ring. Remove from the freezer and fill the ring with raspberry sherbet to form the second layer. Smooth the surface of the dessert and place it back in the freezer for at least 3 hours before decorating and serving.

To Decorate and Serve: At least 2 hours before serving, remove the ring. Using a flexible-blade spatula, spread a third of the Chantilly Cream evenly over the top and sides of the dessert; the cream should form a thin, even layer about ¼ inch (½ cm) thick. Place the remaining cream in a pastry bag fitted with a star-shaped nozzle. Decorate the sides of the dessert with the oval meringues by placing them against the sides of the dessert as shown in the photo. Leave a little space in between the meringues; then, using the cream in the pastry bag, decorate these areas as well as the circumference of the top of the dessert (see photo). Put the dessert back into the freezer until ready to soften in the refrigerator and serve.

Just before taking the dessert to the table, fill the space in the center of the top of the meringue shell with the fresh fruit and spoon over a little fresh fruit sauce made with the same fruit. Serve immediately with a sauceboat of the fresh fruit sauce to accompany the dessert.

To Store: This dessert can be kept in the freezer for up to 2 weeks before decorating and serving; once decorated, the dessert should be served within 12 hours.

Note: A classic when made with Vanilla Ice Cream as a first layer, this dessert is even more enticing when apricot sherbet is used instead.

♙ ♙ ♙

120

Baked Alaska

(Photo page 204)

PREPARATION	1 hour
COOLING TIME	1 hour
COOKING TIME	1 or 2 minutes
FREEZING TIME	4 hours before decorating (see Note)
INGREDIENTS	*For 1 dessert serving 6 to 8* 1 Génoise (Recipe 67) 12 × 8 inches (30 × 20 cm) ½ cup (1.2 d*l*) 28° Sugar Syrup (Recipe 97) ⅓ cup (8 c*l*) kirsch ½ cup (100 g) chopped mixed candied fruits 1 quart (1 *l*) Vanilla Ice Cream (Recipe 103) *For the meringue* 6 egg whites 3 tablespoons granulated sugar Generous ⅔ cup (150 g) granulated sugar 1 cup (150 g) confectioner's sugar *For decoration* Generous ½ cup (50 g) slivered almonds 2 tablespoons (20 g) confectioner's sugar

                              Long serrated knife
                              Oval, metal or oven-proof serving platter, 14 inches
                                 (36 cm) long
                              Several cardboard "rulers"
                              Pastry brush
                              Large plate or sheet of aluminum foil
                              Flexible-blade, metal spatula
                              Large mixing bowl
                              Electric mixer or wire whisk
                              Sifter
                              Wooden spatula
                              Pastry bag with star-shaped nozzle (optional)

Preparing and Filling the Cake: Using a serrated knife, cut off the corners and trim the end of the génoise so that it will be oval shaped and fit easily on the serving platter. Cut the génoise in half, forming two layers. To do this, pile up strips or "rulers" of cardboard on both sides of the cake and about half the height of the cake, lay the blade of the serrated knife on these "rulers" and begin cutting; the rulers will guide the blade of the knife and keep it parallel to the table as you cut.

Lift off the top half of the cake carefully and place it on a large plate or a sheet of aluminum foil. Place the bottom half of the cake on the metal serving platter. Combine the sugar syrup with the kirsch and measure out ⅔ cup (1.5 dl) of the kirsch-flavored syrup. Brush both halves of the cake equally with it; then place both halves in the freezer for at least 1 hour before proceeding to fill the cake with the ice cream.

While the cake is in the freezer, place the candied fruit in a bowl with the remaining kirsch-flavored sugar syrup and let stand.

The Vanilla Ice Cream can be made at this time, or if made previously, it should be placed in the refrigerator to soften so that once the cake comes from the freezer the ice cream will be softened to a "newly made" consistency.

When the ice cream is ready, drain the candied fruit and stir it gently into the ice cream. Take the two halves of the cake from the freezer and spread all of the Vanilla Ice Cream evenly over the bottom half that is on the serving platter. Once this is done, place the other half of the cake on top of the ice cream and place the dessert back in the freezer for at least 4 hours before decorating and serving (see Note).

To Decorate and Serve: Preheat the oven to its maximum temperature or light the broiler, half an hour in advance.

Beat the egg whites until stiff, adding the 3 tablespoons of granulated sugar half way through the beating time. Once the egg whites are stiff, put the remaining granulated sugar and the confectioner's sugar into a sifter and sift onto the beaten whites. Use a spatula to cut and fold the sugar into the egg whites. This step may be done 30 to 45 minutes in advance and the meringue placed in the refrigerator.

Remove the dessert from the freezer and use a flexible blade spatula to spread three quarters of the meringue over the top and sides of the dessert. The dessert should be evenly coated with meringue. Place the remaining meringue in a pastry bag fitted with a star-shaped nozzle and decorate the surface with swirls and lines like those shown in the photo; a simpler solution to decorating is to spread all of the meringue over the top and sides of the dessert, lifting it here and there with the spatula to make peaks. The dessert may be decorated, then placed back in the freezer up to 1 hour before serving.

When ready to serve, sprinkle the dessert with slivered almonds and 2 tablespoons of sifted confectioner's sugar and place in the oven or under the broiler for 1 to 2 minutes before the dessert is to be served. Watch it carefully while it is in the oven; the meringue should be golden brown and the dessert should be served immediately as it comes from the oven.

Note: The success of this dessert depends on the cake and ice cream being very hard before the decoration is added and the dessert is browned; if not hard enough, the ice cream will melt in the oven. For this reason, it is often best to leave the cake and ice cream, once assembled, in the freezer overnight or even several days before it is to be decorated and served.

Variations: When fresh strawberries or raspberries are in season, sprinkle a few over the meringue just before it goes in the oven.

Choosing Chocolates

Two basic kinds of chocolate are called for in this book: semi-sweet (dark) chocolate and milk chocolate. In fact, professionals use a special kind of chocolate called "covering chocolate" for dipping and making chocolate coating. This chocolate contains a very high percent of cocoa butter, which means that the finished chocolates are very shiny. Unfortunately, it is much too difficult to use in home candy making since it must be melted, worked, and then hardened several times before finally being melted and held at a constant temperature—between 86 and 90°F (30 to 32°C)—during the actual coating process.

I have found that using semi-sweet chocolate combined with a little cooking oil or shortening, which is very easy to use (see Recipe 121), gives results that are not quite as spectacular as those of professionals but are nevertheless very satisfying.

Milk chocolate has a very different composition from semi-sweet chocolate because the milk has replaced some of the cocoa, but it can be used exactly like semi-sweet chocolate for making chocolate centers as well as for dipping and making chocolate coating. The choice is simply a matter of taste.

Making Chocolate Truffles

Chocolate truffle cream is not hard to make, but its quality also depends greatly on the use of the best ingredients. The cream, especially, should be perfectly fresh and without any acidity which would make it curdle when brought to a boil.

When making chocolate truffles, it is always best to use a yoghurt thermometer to check the temperature of the truffle cream before shaping it. When shaping the chocolates (usually using a pastry bag), it should be between 68 and 77°F (20 to 25°C), or room temperature. The proportion of chocolate to liquid ingredients in the truffle recipes are those I generally use, but for those who prefer either stiffer or creamier truffles, they can simply increase the amount of chocolate or reduce it, respectively; the more chocolate, the stiffer the truffle cream. In any case, the chocolate is generally broken into small pieces and mixed with the other ingredients away from the heat (see specific instructions in the recipes that follow).

Once the chocolate truffles are made, they should be served within a week. Since they are not coated with a hard chocolate coating, they soften very quickly; store them in the refrigerator and take them out just before serving (they should be eaten within 30 minutes of the time they come from the refrigerator).

121
Chocolate Coating

This chocolate coating is not as shiny nor as thin as that made by professionals. Nevertheless, it is perfectly adapted for home use and permits the making of a great variety of homemade chocolate candies.

PREPARATION	5 minutes
COOKING TIME	10 minutes
COOLING TIME	30 minutes

INGREDIENTS	*For coating 40 to 50 chocolates*
	7 ounces (200 g) semi-sweet chocolate
	   or 7 ounces (200 g) milk chocolate
	2 tablespoons tasteless cooking oil, cocoa butter, *or*
	   melted vegetable shortening

UTENSILS	Small, metal, mixing bowl and small saucepan (*bain-marie) or* double boiler Wooden spoon *or* spatula Yoghurt thermometer Dish towel (optional) Fork Sheet of plastic *or* nonstick parchment paper Knife

Recommendations: If the chocolate coating is made with cooking oil, it will be easier to work with than if it is made with cocoa butter or vegetable shortening.

Also, since the chocolate can be melted and reused several times, you can plan to make a large number of chocolates—double or triple the measurements given here. It won't go bad, and will make it easier later. After coating each batch of candies but before putting the chocolate away, be sure to clean the inside edges of the mixing bowl or double boiler with a plastic scraper.

Melting the Chocolate: Place a little water in a small saucepan or the bottom of a double boiler; then set a mixing bowl in the saucepan to make a *bain-marie* or put the top half of the double boiler in place. The water should not touch the bottom of the bowl or double boiler.

Bring the water to a boil; then remove the *bain-marie* or double boiler from the heat. Break the chocolate into pieces, and place the pieces of chocolate and the oil, cocoa butter, or shortening in the bowl or double boiler. Cover and allow to melt for 2 minutes. Then stir with a wooden spoon or spatula. If there are any hard pieces of chocolate left, cover and wait until all of them have melted completely, stirring occasionally.

Do not leave the *bain-marie* or double boiler on the heat. The water might boil, and although the chocolate will melt faster, it will dry out too much, get too hot, and not make as nice a coating.

Another very important point: Do not let even one drop of water get into the chocolate or it will harden immediately and be completely useless.

Coating the Candies: Check the temperature of the chocolate with a yoghurt thermometer—it should be no more than 90°F (32°C) when used for coating. Allow to cool if necessary.

If it is not too hot, the chocolate may be left over the hot water. It is easier to coat the candies, however, if the top of the double boiler or the mixing bowl is set at a tilt by placing a folded dish towel under one edge of it on the table. The chocolate may be warmed, if necessary, by placing it back over the hot water from time to time.

Drop a candy into the melted chocolate, turn it over with a fork to coat all sides, and then lift it out by placing the fork under it. As you lift it out of the chocolate, make a gentle up and down movement with your wrist so that the excess chocolate on the candy will be pulled back into the chocolate still in the bowl or double boiler. Lightly scrape the bottom of the fork against the edge of the pot or bowl so that the chocolate won't drip; then slide the candy onto a sheet of plastic or nonstick parchment paper with the tip of a knife.

Allow the candies to cool for 30 minutes in the refrigerator before serving.

To Store: The chocolate used for coating will keep for a week in the refrigerator, left simply in the bowl or double boiler in which it was melted.

Note: Any leftover chocolate coating may be molded in a lightly oiled mold or container and eaten like a chocolate bar.

122

Mocha Pleasures

PREPARATION	15 minutes
COOKING TIME	10 minutes
COOLING TIME	30 to 50 minutes
INGREDIENTS	*For 35 truffles* 6½ tablespoons (100 g) crème fraîche *or* heavy cream 3 tablespoons milk 2 teaspoons instant coffee 7 ounces (200 g) semi-sweet chocolate broken into pieces 70 sugar coffee beans
UTENSILS	Saucepan with cover Wooden spoon *or* spatula Wire whisk Yoghurt thermometer Pastry bag with ⅛-inch (3-mm) nozzle 35 individual paper cases

Making the Truffle Cream: Place the crème fraîche or heavy cream in a saucepan and bring to a boil stirring constantly. Then add the milk and bring back to a boil. Remove the saucepan from the heat and add the instant coffee and the chocolate. Cover the pot and save for about 3 minutes to allow the chocolate to melt; after that time, use a wooden spoon or spatula to stir the ingredients until a smooth mixture is formed (this should happen easily at this stage). Leave the truffle cream to cool for about 30 to 50 minutes before shaping.

Making the Truffles: When the truffle cream is ready, beat it lightly about 20 times with a wire whisk, wait 2 minutes, and then spoon it into a pastry bag fitted with a ⅛-inch (3-mm) nozzle. Squeeze enough truffle cream into each paper case to fill it no more than half way, place a sugar coffee bean in the center of each one, and then finish filling the case with truffle cream, topped with another sugar coffee bean. Then place them in the refrigerator to harden before serving.

To Store: Once hardened, the truffles can be placed in a tightly sealed container and kept for a week in the refrigerator.

$\widehat{}$

123

Gatines-Style Chocolate Truffles

(Photo page 211)

PREPARATION	15 minutes
COOKING TIME	5 minutes
COOLING TIME	30 to 50 minutes

INGREDIENTS

For 40 to 50 truffles
6½ tablespoons (100 g) crème fraîche or heavy cream
1½ tablespoons (25 g) honey
1½ tablespoons sweetened condensed milk
5¼ ounces (150 g) milk chocolate, broken into pieces
5¼ ounces (150 g) semi-sweet chocolate, broken into pieces

For decoration
5¼ ounces (150 g) semi-sweet chocolate (for cases)
Either ½ cup (100 g) diced candied pineapple slices *or* ½ cup (50 g) chopped walnuts
50 walnut meats

UTENSILS

Saucepan with cover
Wooden spoon *or* spatula
Mixing bowl and saucepan (*bain-marie*) *or* double boiler
Pastry brush
Pastry bag with ¼-inch (6-mm) *or* ⅜-inch (1 cm) nozzle
50 paper cases
Platter

Making the Truffle Cream: Place the crème fraîche or heavy cream in a saucepan and bring to a boil stirring constantly. Then add the honey and condensed milk and bring back to a boil. Remove from the heat, immediately add the pieces of chocolate, and cover the pot. Leave for 3 minutes to allow the chocolate to melt. Then stir with a wooden spoon or spatula until perfectly smooth (the ingredients should mix easily at this stage). Leave the cream to cool for 30 to 50 minutes before shaping.

212

Making the Truffles: The chocolates can be decorated and garnished with either candied pineapple slices or with walnuts. In any case, before making them, melt 5¼ ounces (150 g) of semi-sweet chocolate in a *bain-marie* or double boiler.

Open the paper cases and place them on a platter. Then, using a pastry brush, coat the inside of each paper case with a thin film of chocolate.

To Garnish and Decorate with Pineapple: Whisk the truffle cream a few times. Then spoon it into a pastry bag fitted with a ¼-inch (6-mm) nozzle and squeeze it out to half fill each of the paper cases. Place a piece of pineapple in the middle of each chocolate, finish filling the paper cases with truffle cream, and then place another piece of pineapple on top to decorate. Place the truffles in the refrigerator to harden.

To Garnish and Decorate with Walnuts: Mix the chopped nuts into the truffle cream. Then spoon the cream into a pastry bag with a ⅜-inch (1-cm) nozzle and squeeze it into the paper cases to fill them. Place a walnut meat on top of each chocolate and place in the refrigerator to harden.

To Store: Once hardened, the truffles can be kept for a week in a tightly sealed container in the refrigerator.

124

Cusenier Chocolate Truffles

(Photo page 211)

PREPARATION	30 minutes
COOKING TIME	10 minutes
COOLING TIME	30 minutes for the truffle cream 40 minutes to 1 hour to harden
INGREDIENTS	*For 50 truffles* ½ cup (120 g) crème fraîche or heavy cream 10½ ounces (300 g) semi-sweet chocolate, broken into pieces 2 tablespoons Cusenier or other orange-flavored liqueur *For the Coating* 7 ounces (200 g) milk chocolate 2 teaspoons cooking oil *For decoration* ⅓ cup (50 g) confectioner's sugar

Saucepan with cover
Wooden spoon or spatula
Mixing bowl
Yoghurt thermometer
Baking sheet
Nonstick parchment paper
Pastry bag with ⅝-inch (1.5-cm) nozzle
Shallow dish *or* soup bowl
50 individual paper cases
Fork

Making the Truffle Cream: Place the crème fraîche or heavy cream in a saucepan and bring to a boil stirring constantly. Then remove from the heat and immediately add the chocolate. Cover the saucepan and leave for 5 minutes to allow the chocolate to melt. After the time is up, stir the chocolate with a wooden spoon or spatula to make a smooth cream; then pour the mixture into a mixing bowl and stir in the liqueur little by little. Leave the truffle cream to cool in the refrigerator for 30 minutes, removing it from the refrigerator so it will not cool off too much.

Making the Truffles: Line a baking sheet with nonstick parchment paper (stick the corners down with a little of the truffle cream). Spoon the cooled truffle cream into a pastry bag fitted with a ⅝-inch (1.5-cm) nozzle, and squeeze it out in long lines on the parchment paper. Place the baking sheet in the refrigerator for 40 minutes to 1 hour to harden the chocolate; then remove from the refrigerator and cut the lines of chocolate into pieces 1¼ inches (3 cm) long. Place the pieces back in the refrigerator while preparing the chocolate coating.

Melt the chocolate for the coating and add the oil as described in Recipe 121 for Chocolate Coating.

Place the confectioner's sugar in a shallow dish or soup bowl.

Open the paper cases and place them on a platter.

When everything is ready for coating the chocolates, remove the chocolates 10 at a time from the refrigerator, leaving the others in the refrigerator while coating the first 10, and so on. Dip a chocolate in the melted chocolate as described in the recipe for Chocolate Coating (page 209), then lift it out, and place in the confectioners' sugar. When 10 of the chocolates have been dipped, roll them in the confectioner's sugar, using a fork, and place them in individual paper cases.

When all the truffles have been coated and decorated, place them in the refrigerator to harden.

To Store: The truffles will keep for 1 week in a tightly sealed container in the refrigerator, although it is best to place them in a little extra confectioner's sugar if keeping them for any length of time.

PREPARATION	15 minutes, one day in advance
	15 minutes for the truffle cream
COOLING TIME	Approximately 30 minutes
INGREDIENTS	*For 50 truffles*
	Scant 1½ cups (3 d*l*) water
	Scant ½ cup (80 g) raisins
	1½ tablespoons rum
	Generous ½ cup (125 g) crème fraîche or heavy cream
	9 ounces (250 g) milk chocolate, broken into pieces
UTENSILS	Small saucepan
	Small bowl with cover
	Large saucepan with cover
	Yoghurt thermometer
	Wooden spoon *or* spatula
	Knife
	Pastry bag with star-shaped nozzle
	50 paper cases
	Platter *or* baking sheet

Preliminary Preparations: The day before making the truffle cream, bring the water to a boil in a saucepan, remove from the heat, and stir in the raisins. Leave the raisins to swell in the water for 15 minutes, then drain completely, and place them in a bowl with the rum. Cover the bowl and leave it at room temperature until the next day.

Making the Truffle Cream: When ready to make the truffle cream, place the crème fraîche or heavy cream in a saucepan and bring to a boil, stirring constantly. Once the cream boils, remove the saucepan from the heat and add the pieces of chocolate. Cover the pot and leave for 3 minutes to allow the chocolate to melt. Then stir the mixture with a wooden spoon or spatula until perfectly smooth (the ingredients should mix easily at this stage). Leave the truffle cream to cool for 30 minutes in the refrigerator before proceeding to shape the chocolates; remove it from the refrigerator at the end of this time so that it won't get too cold.

Making the Truffles: Open the paper cases and place them on a platter or baking sheet.

Take about 50 whole raisins and save them for decorating the truffles. Use a knife to chop the remaining raisins; then whisk them into the truffle cream. After whisking, leave the truffle cream at room temperature for 2 minutes. Then spoon it into a pastry bag fitted with a star-shaped nozzle and squeeze out the cream to fill the paper cases. Top each truffle with one of the whole raisins reserved earlier (see photo). Place the chocolates in the refrigerator to harden.

To Store: Once the chocolates have hardened they will keep in a tightly sealed container for 1 week in the refrigerator.

126

Calvados-Flavored Chocolate Truffles

(Photo page 211)

PREPARATION	30 minutes
COOKING TIME	10 minutes
COOLING TIME	30 minutes to 1½ hours
INGREDIENTS	*For 35 truffles*
	7 ounces (200 g) milk chocolate
	3 tablespoons (50 g) crème fraîche or heavy cream
	2½ tablespoons (35 g) granulated sugar
	2 tablespoons calvados (see Note)
	For decoration (Method 1)
	Scant ½ cup (50 g) cocoa powder
	For decoration (Method 2)
	3½ ounces (100 g) milk chocolate
	3½ ounces (100 g) semi-sweet chocolate
	2 teaspoons tasteless cooking oil

2 mixing bowls and saucepans *(bains-marie)* *or* 2 double
                boilers
            Wooden spoon or spatula
            Ordinary spoon
            Mixing bowl
            Small saucepan
            Pastry bag with ⅛-inch (3-mm) nozzle (optional)
            Baking sheet
            Nonstick parchment paper
            Vegetable grater with large holes
            Yoghurt thermometer
            Dish towel
            Fork
            Sheet of plastic *or* nonstick parchment paper
            Knife
            35 paper cases
            Platter

Making the Truffle Cream: Melt the 7 ounces of milk chocolate to be used in the truffle cream in a *bain-marie* or double boiler as described for Chocolate Coating (page 208).

Place the crème fraîche or heavy cream in a small saucepan, bring to a boil, stir in the granulated sugar, and then pour this mixture onto the melted chocolate, stirring to mix well. The resulting mixture should be perfectly smooth. Stir in the calvados and leave the truffle cream to cool to room temperature.

Making the Truffles: There are two ways of making and serving the truffles made with the cream given here.

Method 1.   The first and simplest method is to whisk the cooled truffle cream lightly, then spoon it into a pastry bag fitted with a ⅛-inch (3-mm) nozzle, and squeeze it out into the paper cases. Then dust the surface of each truffle with a little cocoa powder.

Method 2.   The second method of shaping the truffles is to leave the truffle cream in the refrigerator to stiffen slightly for 30 minutes so that it can be shaped into balls.

Line a baking sheet with nonstick parchment paper (stick the corners of the paper down with a little of the truffle cream). Then either spoon the truffle cream into a pastry bag fitted with a ⅛-inch (3-mm) nozzle and squeeze it out onto the parchment paper to make about 35 walnut-sized mounds, or take a teaspoon of the cream and scrape it onto the paper with a second teaspoon to form the mounds. Place the baking sheet in the refrigerator to harden the chocolate for 30 to 50 minutes.

Meanwhile, using a vegetable grater with large holes, grate the milk chocolate used for the decoration into a shallow dish or soup plate.

Prepare the chocolate coating using the amounts of semi-sweet chocolate and cooking oil given here but following the directions in Recipe 121 for Chocolate Coating.

Open the paper cases and place them on a platter.

When the mounds of chocolate have hardened, take one from the refrigerator and roll it rapidly between the palms of your hands to form a ball and then quickly dip it in the chocolate as described in Recipe 121 for Chocolate Coating. Lift the truffle out of the chocolate and place it in the plate of chocolate shavings. When five truffles are in the plate, roll them in the shavings using a fork, turning and coating them with shavings on all sides; then lift them out of the shavings and place them in individual paper cases. Continue in this manner until all the truffles have been dipped and coated with shavings.

To Store: The finished truffles will keep for 1 week in a tightly closed box in the refrigerator.

Note: An interesting variation of this recipe can be made with Scotch whiskey instead of calvados. These "Scotch truffles" are made exactly as described here by replacing the calvados with Scotch and using semi-sweet chocolate rather than milk chocolate when making the truffle cream.

♟

127

Norman-Style Chocolate Truffles

PREPARATION	15 minutes
COOKING TIME	10 minutes
COOLING TIME	30 minutes
INGREDIENTS	*For 40 to 50 truffles or 1 cup (275 g) Norman-Style Truffle Cream* 3 tablespoons (50 g) crème fraîche or heavy cream 5 teaspoons (25 g) butter ¼ a vanilla bean, split lengthwise ¼ cup (50 g) granulated sugar 1 egg yolk 2¾ ounces (80 g) semi-sweet chocolate broken into pieces 2¾ ounces (80 g) milk chocolate broken into pieces *For decoration* 50 caramelized hazelnuts

Large saucepan with cover
Wire whisk
Mixing bowl
Wooden spoon *or* spatula
Baking sheet
Nonstick parchment paper
Yoghurt thermometer
Pastry bag with star-shaped nozzle
50 paper cases

Making the Truffle Cream: Place the crème fraîche or heavy cream in a saucepan and bring to a boil, stirring constantly with a wire whisk. Then add the butter, vanilla bean, and half of the sugar. Continue whisking over the heat until the mixture comes back to a boil; then remove from the heat.

Place the remaining sugar in a mixing bowl with the egg yolk and whisk until the mixture whitens; this will take about 30 seconds, and all the sugar should dissolve. Pour the beaten egg yolk–sugar mixture into the saucepan with the other ingredients, whisking rapidly to combine all the ingredients together. Place the saucepan over medium heat for about 5 seconds, whisking constantly; then remove from the heat. Take out the vanilla bean, add the chocolate, and cover the pot. Leave for 3 minutes to allow the chocolate to melt, and then stir with a wooden spoon or spatula to make a smooth mixture (this should be easy to do at this stage). Leave the cream to cool for 30 minutes in the refrigerator, then remove it so it will not be too cold to form the truffles.

Making the Truffles: Cover a baking sheet with a piece of nonstick parchment paper (stick the corners of the paper down with a little of the truffle cream). Spoon the truffle cream into a pastry bag fitted with a star-shaped nozzle and squeeze it out into about 40 to 50 rose-like mounds. Top each little mound with a caramelized hazelnut. Then place the truffles in the refrigerator to harden. Once hard, place each truffle in an individual paper case to serve or store.

To Store: Once hardened, the truffles can be kept in a tightly sealed container for 1 week in the refrigerator.

Uses: The Norman-Style Truffle Cream is also used to make Wafer Rounds Filled with Truffle Cream (Recipe 128).

128

Wafer Rounds Filled with Truffle Cream

PREPARATION	30 minutes
BAKING TIME	12 minutes
INGREDIENTS	*For 50 to 60 petits fours* ¾ cup (200 g) Vanilla Wafer Batter (Recipe 113) Scant 1½ cups (400 g) Norman-Style Truffle Cream (Recipe 127)
UTENSILS	60 individual paper cases (preferably brown nonstick parchment paper) Baking sheet Pastry bag A ⅛-inch (3-mm) round nozzle A star-shaped nozzle

Baking the Wafer Rounds and Filling the Cases: Preheat the oven to 400°F (200°C).

If brown nonstick parchment paper cases are not available, use ordinary white paper cases and brush each one with a little melted butter; place the paper cases on a baking sheet.

Fill a pastry bag fitted with a ⅛-inch (3-mm) nozzle with the wafer batter and squeeze enough batter into each cut, using a spiral motion, to fill it by about a third. Place the baking sheet in the oven and bake for 12 minutes (the paper will straighten up around the batter when baking).

When done, remove the wafers from the oven and leave to cool in their cups before filling them (see photo). To fill the cups, pour the truffle cream into a pastry bag fitted with a star-shaped nozzle and squeeze enough truffle cream into each cup to fill it.

To Store: Once baked, but before filling the paper cases with the truffle cream, the wafer rounds can be kept in their cases in a cookie box for up to a week, but once the truffle cream has been added, the chocolates can be kept for only 24 hours in the refrigerator.

129
Eiffel Towers

PREPARATION	**20 to 30 minutes**
COOKING TIME	**10 minutes**
COOLING TIME	**15 minutes**
INGREDIENTS	*For 40 to 50 candies* 1 cup (160 g) shelled hazelnuts ⅓ cup (70 g) granulated sugar 4½ teaspoons water ½ a vanilla bean, split in half lengthwise *For Chocolate coating* 7 ounces (200 g) semi-sweet chocolate 4½ teaspoons tasteless cooking oil
UTENSILS	Baking sheet Drum sieve, fine mesh strainer, *or* clean dish towel Platter Nonstick parchment paper Small saucepan Straight-edged, wooden spatula Small mixing bowl and saucepan (*bain-marie*) *or* double boiler

Preliminary Preparations: Preheat the oven to 370°F (175°C).

Place the hazelnuts on a baking sheet and roast in the oven for 7 minutes. Then to remove their skins, rub the nuts against the mesh of a drum sieve or fine mesh strainer or wrap them in a clean dish towel and rub them together vigorously. Leave the oven on for later use.

Remove the baking sheet from the oven and oil it lightly.

Place a sheet of nonstick parchment paper on a platter or on a second baking sheet. This is for placing the finished candies on.

Making the Candies: In the saucepan, place the sugar, water, and vanilla bean. Bring to a boil and boil rapidly uncovered for 3 minutes or until the syrup reaches the Firm Ball stage (see page 34), 244°F (118°C).

Remove the saucepan from the heat and add the hazelnuts. Stir gently with a straight-edged, wooden spatula—the mixture will become grainy and look somewhat like sand. This takes about 30 seconds to a minute.

Place the saucepan back over moderate heat, stirring constantly. Gradually the sugar will begin to melt again and caramelize. Roll the nuts around in the sugar to coat them, and scrape off any sugar that sticks to the spatula against the sides of the saucepan. Do not allow the mixture to smoke—lower the heat if necessary. When the nuts are done they will be coated lightly with caramel and make a dry clicking sound as they hit each other.

Pour the coated nuts out onto the oiled baking sheet. Oil your fingers and stick 3 nuts together, then place a fourth one on top of them, forming a little pyramid (see photo). Place the finished "towers" on the parchment paper.

During the time it takes to form the candies, the ones left on the baking sheet may dry and harden, so place the baking sheet back in the oven from time to time, to keep the caramel soft and sticky.

Allow the finished candies to cool for 15 minutes at room temperature (not in the refrigerator).

Coating the Candies: Melt the chocolate, add the oil, and dip the candies into it to coat them as described in Recipe 121 for Chocolate Coating. Place the finished chocolates in the refrigerator for 15 minutes to harden the chocolate before serving.

To Store: The chocolate-coated Eiffel Towers will keep for 2 weeks in a tightly closed box in the refrigerator. The candies may be eaten without being coated with chocolate. In this case they will keep for 2 weeks in a tightly closed box in a dry place. Do not place them in the refrigerator or the caramel will absorb humidity and become sticky.

‿‿‿ (chef hats decorative)

130
Chocolate Thistles
(Photo page 226)

PREPARATION	30 minutes
COOKING TIME	5 minutes
COOLING TIME	40 minutes to 2 hours

INGREDIENTS

For 50 to 60 candies
1 generous cup tightly packed (320 g) white or green Almond Paste (Recipe 18)
Confectioner's sugar or potato starch to sprinkle work surface
2 tablespoons 28° Sugar Syrup (Recipe 97) *or* 1 tablespoon granulated sugar dissolved in 1 tablespoon hot water

For chocolate coating
7 ounces (200 g) semi-sweet chocolate
Cocoa powder (optional)

For truffle cream
¼ cup (60 g) crème fraîche or heavy cream
5¼ ounces (150 g) semi-sweet chocolate

UTENSILS

Mixing bowl and small saucepan (*bain-marie*) *or* double boiler
Rolling pin
Ruler
Pastry bag with ⅝-inch (1.5-cm) nozzle
Pastry brush
Knife
60 individual paper cases
Platter

Making the Rolls: **Make the truffle cream according to the directions in Recipe 122. Set aside and allow to cool, while you roll out the almond paste.**

Sprinkle the work surface with confectioner's sugar or potato starch. Then roll out the Almond Paste into a rectangle 8 by 12 inches (20 by 30 cm). Trim the edges to make them square and divide the rectangle lengthwise into three bands, approximately 2½ inches (6 cm) wide each.

225

When the truffle cream has cooled to the proper temperature, fill the pastry bag with it and press out a long sausage of truffle cream about a third of the way in from one edge of each band of almond paste (see photo).

With a pastry brush, moisten the almond paste on both sides of each "sausage" with the sugar syrup.

Starting from the edge furthest away from the "sausage," roll the almond paste over the truffle cream pressing the second edge lightly over the first to make it stick (see photo); then turn the finished roll over so that the seam is on the bottom.

Place the three finished rolls in the refrigerator for 1 hour or in the freezer for 20 minutes.

Coating the Rolls and Cutting: Melt the chocolate in a *bain-marie* or double boiler as described in Recipe 121 for Chocolate Coating—make sure the chocolate does not heat past 95°F (35°C).

Remove the rolls from the refrigerator and, using a pastry brush, paint them with the chocolate, starting on the bottom side and tapping lightly with the brush to make little spikes like those on a thistle. While the chocolate is still soft, a little cocoa may be sprinkled over it.

When coating the rolls, the chocolate may begin to cool too much; if this happens and it begins to harden on the brush, simply heat it until it reaches 90°F (32°C) again, leaving the brush in it so that the chocolate on it will melt as well.

When the rolls are all coated with chocolate, place them in the refrigerator for 10 to 15 minutes or until the chocolate has hardened completely.

While the rolls are cooling, arrange the paper cases on a platter.

When the chocolate coating is hard, remove the rolls from the refrigerator and cut them into slices about ⅝ inch (1.5 cm) thick with a sharp knife that has been dipped into hot water and wiped dry. Place each slice in a paper case and keep the chocolate thistles in the refrigerator until ready to serve.

To Store: The finished chocolate thistles will keep for 2 weeks in a tightly closed box in the refrigerator.

131

Grilled Slivered Almonds

PREPARATION	10 minutes
BAKING TIME	5 to 10 minutes
INGREDIENTS	*For 1 generous cup (100 g) almonds* 4½ teaspoons granulated sugar 2 tablespoons water 1 generous cup (100 g) slivered almonds 1 teaspoon orange-flower water
UTENSILS	Baking sheet Nonstick parchment paper Small saucepan Wooden spoon Mixing bowl Fork Serving platter or baking sheet (for cooling)

To Flavor and Brown the Almonds: Preheat the oven to 350°F (175°C).

Line a baking sheet with nonstick parchment paper.

Place the sugar and water in a small saucepan and heat enough to dissolve the sugar.

Place the almonds in a mixing bowl, add the orange-flower water, and then pour over the sugar syrup, stirring gently so as not to break the almonds.

Pour the coated almonds out onto the baking sheet and spread them out with the aid of a fork or spoon as much as possible, so that they form an even layer on the baking sheet. Place them in the oven and, after 5 minutes have passed, check to see that the almonds are browning properly. Not all ovens brown evenly, so check often, and as soon as any of the almonds have browned, remove them from the oven with a fork; continue baking the remaining almonds, removing them as they brown.

As they come from the oven, spread the almonds onto a cold baking sheet or a serving platter to cool; detach them from one another as much as possible so that they do not stick together when cooling.

Uses: Grilled slivered almonds are used to sprinkle over and decorate numerous ice cream desserts; they are also used in some of our chocolate recipes.

To Store: Once they have cooled completely, the almonds can be kept in a tightly sealed container in a dry place for up to 1 month.

132

Caramelized Almonds or Hazelnuts

PREPARATION	15 minutes
COOKING TIME	10 minutes
INGREDIENTS	*For 10½ ounces (300 g) caramelized almonds*
	1⅓ cups (200 g) shelled almonds
	½ cup (100 g) granulated sugar
	2 tablespoons water
	½ a vanilla bean, split in half lengthwise
	1 tablespoon (15 g) butter
	For ½ pound (250 g) caramelized hazelnuts
	1⅓ cup (200 g) shelled hazelnuts
	Generous ⅓ cup (75 g) granulated sugar
	1½ tablespoons water
	½ a vanilla bean, split in half lengthwise
	1 tablespoon (15 g) butter
UTENSILS	Baking sheet
	Drum sieve, fine grill, *or* clean cloth
	Medium saucepan
	Candy thermometer (optional)
	Wooden spoon *or* spatula
	2 forks

Preliminary Preparations: If using hazelnuts, remove their thin brown skins as follows.

Preheat the oven to 350°F (175°C).

Spread the hazelnuts on the baking sheet and heat them in the oven for 7 minutes. Remove them from the oven and place them on a drum sieve or fine grill. Remove their skins by rubbing them against it. The skin can also be removed by wrapping them in a clean cloth or dish towel and rubbing the nuts together inside it.

It is unnecessary to remove the skins from the almonds; on the contrary, their skin gives a very good taste to this candy.

Caramelizing the Nuts: Place the sugar, water, and vanilla bean in a saucepan. Bring slowly to a boil, stirring until the sugar has melted; then boil rapidly for 2 to 3 minutes or until the syrup reaches the Firm Ball stage (see page 34), 244°F (118°C).

Remove the saucepan from the heat and add the nuts to the syrup. Stir gently with a wooden spoon or spatula to coat all the nuts—the mixture will begin to look sandy. Continue stirring gently for 30 seconds.

Place the saucepan back over moderate heat, stirring gently. The sugar will slowly melt and caramelize. As this happens, roll the nuts in the caramel with the wooden spoon or spatula; the nuts will begin to color and make a dry clicking sound as they touch each other. Do not let the mixture smoke—if it does, immediately lower the heat.

When all the sugar has caramelized and the nuts are coated, remove the saucepan from the heat and stir in the butter. When the butter has been mixed in, pour the contents of the saucepan out onto an oiled baking sheet, spreading it out with the wooden spoon.

Allow the caramelized nuts to cool for a few minutes, using two forks to stir them and turn them over. When the caramel has hardened, separate any nuts that are sticking to each other.

To serve: The caramelized almonds or hazelnuts can be eaten as they are or coated with chocolate (see Recipe 121 for Chocolate Coating).

To Store: The caramelized nuts will keep for 2 weeks in an airtight box in the refrigerator or in a cool dry place. If kept in the refrigerator, you must be sure that the box they are kept in is *very* tightly closed; if exposed to humidity, the nuts will soften and taste stale.

Powdered Caramelized Almonds: Caramelized almonds are often ground and used to flavor and decorate desserts. Once they are prepared as described above, simply reduce them to a coarse powder in a heavy duty blender or a food processor. *Ed.*

INDEX